A VISIT TO FLANDERS,

IN JULY, 1815,

BEING CHIEFLY AN ACCOUNT

OF THE

Field of Waterloo,

WITH A SHORT SKETCH OF

ANTWERP AND BRUSSELS,

AT THAT TIME

OCCUPIED BY THE WOUNDED OF BOTH ARMIES.

BY

JAMES SIMPSON, ESQ.

My Country!......................................
................I can feel thy fortunes, and partake
Thy joys and sorrows with as true a heart
As any.................................... COWPER.

The Naval & Military Press Ltd

Published by

The Naval & Military Press Ltd
Unit 5 Riverside, Brambleside
Bellbrook Industrial Estate
Uckfield, East Sussex
TN22 1QQ England

Tel: +44 (0)1825 749494

www.naval-military-press.com
www.nmarchive.com

In reprinting in facsimile from the original, any imperfections are inevitably reproduced and the quality may fall short of modern type and cartographic standards.

PREFACE.

The following pages are a part of a series of notes, written during a tour through Holland, Flanders, and France, in July, August, and September last.

Their publication in the present form was suggested by a persuasion of the interest of every circumstance connected with Waterloo; and by a feeling that my own estimate of that wonderful field, however high before, has been incalculably exalted by my visit to its scene, and my intercourse with many of its gallant soldiers. Bold would the writer be who should presume to think, that any thing originating with himself, could deepen the public impression of Waterloo. But any one who felt as he ought, may " tell the tale, as it was told to him," encouraged by the assurance, that an intelligible account of what he could not fail to see and hear, must possess intrinsic value enough to plead his apology for laying it before the public.

My information was drawn from the most authentic sources, either on the memorable spot, or subsequently in Paris, where it was my good fortune to be much in the society of military men.

As I have referred occasionally to the accounts of the battle by the Duke of Wellington, Marshal Blucher, General Alava, Bonaparte, and Marshal Ney, it has been judged right to append these important documents.

The engraved Plan is a copy of one published in Brussels, from accurate survey; and by far the most satisfactory which I have seen.

My description is necessarily limited and partial. It is a tourist's passing sketch, not a circumstantial military detail. I have not a doubt, that much as I have heard, I have still a great deal more to hear. If, therefore, in the very inadequate account which I have ventured to give of some striking incidents, I have omitted any of the actors immediately concerned, I have no other plea than the imperfection, so far, of my knowledge. At the same time, the mere possibility of such omission would be no good reason for suppressing any part of the well vouched *positive* information which I did obtain.

It was to be expected that I should hear more of the minuter history of the regiments of my own country, than of those in which I did not enjoy the advantage of a single acquaintance; and I am quite aware, that my narrative has thereby contracted a strong *national* character. But, on the other hand, besides attempting to convey, what I intensely feel, an unqualified impression generally of the valour and constancy of the " Waterloo men," of the two sister kingdoms, I have recited, with unfeigned delight, several anecdotes to their exclusive honour; and, further, I have reason to know, that I have said nothing of the soldiers of Scotland, but what is borne out by the universal testimony of friends and foes. I have, therefore, submitted this observation more in the spirit of explanation than apology.

Edinburgh, 30th Oct. 1815.

CONTENTS.

	Page
ANTWERP,	1
BRUSSELS,	27
VISIT TO THE FIELD,	52
CONCLUSION,	127

APPENDIX.

British Account of the Battle of Waterloo—London Gazette Extraordinary, ... 141

Prussian Account——Official Report of Marshal Blucher, ... 152

Spanish Account——Dispatch from General Miguel Alava 162

French Official Account, ... 171

Marshal Ney's Observations on the Battle, ... 180

CHAPTER I.

ANTWERP.

Caserne de Facon, one of the hospitals of wounded British—La Corderie, the hospital of wounded French—Citadel—Convicts in chains—Wounded officers—Highlanders in Antwerp—Docks of Napoleon—View from the tower of the Cathedral—Streets and houses of Antwerp—Cathedral, and blanks left for Rubens' pictures expected to be restored.

After a four days passage from Leith, and a short but delightful tour through the most interesting part of Holland,—viz. from Rotterdam by the Hague, Leyden, and Haarlem, to Amsterdam; and south again by Utrecht and Breda,—I entered Flanders at Le Coin D'Argent on the 27th July; and in a few hours arrived at Antwerp.

Much of the novel feeling of first treading the long interdicted Continent had worn off; and I had even become so much familiarized, as to travel many a very straight mile on Napoleon's great chaussée of granite, with hardly a glance bestowed upon the little varying scenery on either side of it. But there did occur places in our progress so fertile in interesting associations, so identified with our impressions of French presence and power, so recently the lair of the dreadful monster just hunted down, that it was impossible to approach them without the most engrossing sensations; made up of avidity to survey them closely; a certain increase of pulse on entering their lately implacable gates; and a large share of national pride because a visit, so long dangerous, is now *made* safe; and the visitors received with a sort of consideration even, on account of their country.

To no place of strength and importance do these observations apply with more force than to Antwerp; a name which we have long connected with an undefined idea of danger to England; the greater, that we were long in ignorance of its nature and extent; but which we knew to be the favourite, jealously guarded, and almost mysterious *officina*, where something very tremendous was forging against us by an enemy, whose means invariably exceeded our utmost calculations. These considerations much increased the intensity of my gaze at the broad ditches, lines, and bastions of that almost impregnable place; and gave a double effect in imagination to the cannon which pointed on the long bridges; till, on arriving at the gate, I saw the first proof of the satisfactory change of times, a guard of the 25th regiment of our own trust-worthy country.

After the verification of my passport at the office of the police, I was much surprised to hear my name called out in very friendly English, as I was crossing the great square in front of the Hotel de Ville. To my great satisfaction, I saw my friends, Dr. Somerville, inspector general of military hospitals in Scotland, and Dr. Thomson, professor of military surgery in Edinburgh; who had, with an enterprise and benevolence most creditable to themselves, set out on a few hours notice, for this country of wounds, on hearing of the battle of Waterloo. The great body of wounded at Brussels, had for a considerable time occupied their attention; and they had now come to Antwerp in prosecution of their investigations. As they had visited a near relative of my own, severely wounded at Quatre Bras, captain in the first foot guards,—my first inquiry was naturally about his progress; when, equally to my surprise and satisfaction, I was informed, that he had a short time before obtained leave to depart for England, in a fair way of recovery; and they had heard of his arrival in London.

The ordinary permanent objects of the traveller's attention in Flanders and France, suffered an undoubted postponement, in this eventful year, to the marvels of the juncture of which these countries have been the scene.

* Now created *grenadier guards*, in reward for their having defeated the grenadiers of the French imperial guard.

We were now actually in the region of Waterloo; and with an interest in its wondrous theme growing as we approached it. We had now reached the first city where the details of its only yesterday horrors, sufferings, and glories, banished every other topic of conversation. Some thousands of the wounded actually in Antwerp,—many public buildings converted into hospitals,—and many more private houses devoted to the same use,—with all that the brave sufferers loved to relate each of his own share of the great day,—it was in effect to be in the field itself, to be at this time in Antwerp; and the interest of seeing the sufferers was enhanced by being in the company of two of their most skilful, zealous, and justly popular friends.

A higher order of duty than that which prompts a visit merely of sympathy and admiration to the brave in the comparative comfort of a well regulated hospital, would urge one into the midst of the newly created horrors of a field of battle to contribute a mite of aid to mitigate anguish or save life. The impulse would be still stronger than that with which we are hurried to the scene of a shocking accident. Yet it is not uncommon to wonder, how any one can resolve to approach such a scene, where there is the harrowing spectacle of a deluge of blood and heaps of slain, with a multitude of wretched sufferers, writhing and shrieking with agony; added to a kind of horrific idea of the usual process of murdering the unresisting wounded, and plundering and stripping the slain, all legitimately and unavoidably proceeding. Fortunately for our countrymen, Brussels, where they had steady friends, was within a few miles; and many a soldier owed his life to the speedy resort of individuals to the dreadful scene.

It would have been only less blame-worthy than passing them by in the field, to decline an opportunity of visiting in hospital a large body of the very men who had purchased with their limbs, and with their ease for life, the mighty victory with which the whole world resounded.—And no degree of interest can be imagined more intense, than the absolute presence of so striking a feature of the battle as its wounded—with the idea that their sufferings are every day diminishing, and that they are reaping the advantages of a matured system of skill and care, not exceeded in any branch of the multifarious economy of the great country which their firmness and valour has made to triumph. Many a zealous, patient, and undiscouraged medical labourer in the hospitals, with perhaps the gratitude of his patients or his own reflections his only reward, has been heard to regret that the country knows so little of, or cares so little for those noble monuments of the combination, the genius, the skill, and the benevolence of the professors of the healing art. There is no course more certain to a just and high estimate of our country, than an introduction to the interior economy of its grander institutions, civil and military. There is a healthy vigour in every branch, which refers all to one sustaining root of freedom, of light, and of energy; nor is there any better foundation for true patriotism, than an extended knowledge of their wonderful detail.

Something, if possible, beyond the average care for the sick and hurt, appeared to me to animate all ranks of medical men, for the wounded of Waterloo; and their zeal made no distinction between their countrymen and their enemies.

I accompanied my friends to an hospital of 800 British wounded, which they visited in the evening. Nothing could be better fitted for its purpose. One of the finest barracks perhaps in Europe, called the *Caserne de Facon*, intended by Bonaparte for the destined plunderers of London, was immediately available for the comfortable reception of their wounded conquerors. The latter were further indebted to him for the industry with which he had converted all the convents of Antwerp into barracks; nothing could be more convenient and satisfactory, than their easy conversion into hospitals, with the best possible accommodation. There was no end, through my whole tour, to the occurrence of striking examples of that *reversal* of French *destinies*, which the times had produced.

The scene was now entirely divested of its more horrifying features. A general air of comfort and comparative ease was apparent in the accommodations and clothing of the sufferers; and the satisfactory assurance was superadded, that in general they were doing well. There was therefore nothing to prevent the casual visitor from experiencing the peculiar and rare interest of the scene, and connecting it with the field of battle. In all the variety of their honourable marks of that day, the presence of a large body of the wounded of Waterloo was certainly very impressive; nor could any thing be imagined more striking than the sight of their beds, and bandages, and crutches; except actually that of the graves of the slain, on the memorable field itself. We knew that the intended poet of Waterloo was shortly to visit Antwerp and Brussels; and anticipated much from his seeing the wounded.—In the variety of aspects in which the scene would appear to different descriptions of visitors, its poetical features are not the least striking; and combining the affecting spectacle with the field where the ruin was wrought, such a poet could not have failed in a description of the utmost beauty and pathos.—It needed not poetical inspiration, however, to feel intensely the occasion; —and hard would his heart be in a panoply of ingratitude, who could have gone through the ranges of the beds, and seen so many brave men unable to rise, so many limping or creeping about; so many arms in slings and heads bound up; and withal, such perfect patience and order; and glanced in thought at the stupendous boon to mankind, of which this scene of suffering was the price, without a tribute of emotion almost overpowering.

To many of them whom I was assured it did not disturb, there was no resisting the temptation of speaking. A stranger was a kind of novelty to them; and soon learning that I was very recently from home, they were most naturally solicitous to know, that their deeds and their sufferings, were duly appreciated and sympathised with—" What do they say of us at home ?" was several times asked. And a most liberal assurance, that their unequalled merit had ample justice done to it by their countrymen, was very gratifying to them. Out of doors, in a large courtyard, were great numbers of the more slightly hurt and the convalescent; and we were enabled to distinguish our own countrymen by their bonnets. We had them about us in numbers, the moment they heard Scotland mentioned. It was a great refreshment, they said, to hear its name. " They hoped they had not disgraced it." To a man, however, they rejected any exclusive praise on their own account: " They did no more than their duty; and so did every regiment which was there."

The contentment and cheerfulness of these brave men, was very affecting. Every one gave an answer, in which there was resignation or hope, to inquiries how they were; and there was a decency of demeanor and good order, which strongly marked the reasonableness and good sense of the respectable soldiery of our country.

Beyond the citadel, is La Corderie, a building 1300 feet long, constructed by Bonaparte, as a rope work, to give space for the cable of a first rate ship of war. It is fitted up as the hospital of about 1500 of his wounded soldiers, prisoners of war.

A very different feeling from the mingled pity and admiration, with which our own wounded countrymen were visited,—a little hesitation in mingling with these ferocious and exasperated men was not unnatural; but, as a moment of the reality shewed, very unnecessary. Insult was certainly the utmost which a stranger apprehended; but even this had no place, where all were engrossed with their own sufferings; humbled in a consciousness of their irretrievable defeat; and withal, under excellent surveillance and discipline. The whole interminable length of the place was open; and the beds were arranged in four rows, from end to end. We walked generally unnoticed by their occupiers, up and down the lanes between; and equally disregarded, frequently stept over a bed, or passed between two, when going from one passage to another. It was impossible to imagine two extremes of human lot more strikingly contrasted, yet more forcibly associated, than the spectacle which these unfortunate enthusiasts now presented, and their confidence, fury, and presumption but yesterday in the battle; their submissive tranquillity in their flannel gowns and caps, and their noise and cuirasses the other day.

Many cases, however, were such as to stifle all the feelings or associations now described, and substitute unmingled pity in their stead. Death was at work here, much more manifestly than we had observed among the English wounded; numberless faces, as we passed along, seemed hardly to retain signs of life;

a sight tenfold aggravated, when its concomitant idea presented itself, that nature had maintained a struggle with anguish for a whole month, to yield in the end, in circumstances, compared to which, instant death in the field was happiness. The cases in the French hospital, were almost all worse than those in the British; this was especially true of the sabre wounds, a circumstance which was attributed to the superior physical force of the British arm, nerved by revenge for the cruelties of the enemy, which it may be believed were not hid from the men, added to the enthusiasm of pursuit when the day was decided; but in truth, much more naturally resulting from the circumstance, of most of the slightly wounded having found means to escape from the field. It was our fate to witness, as we passed, the actual termination of one poor soldier's sufferings; a moment of deliverance to him, but making an impression on the unpractised beholder, never to be forgotten. We had observed a very miserable looking priest, with his book, visiting several parts of the ward; and now saw him fixed with folded hands, muttering a prayer at the foot of one of the beds, where the clothes were thrown over the face of the occupier. The latter had that moment breathed his last, after dreadful sufferings.

We stood uncovered to hear, and pay becoming respect to their ceremony of blessing the dead. The hourly report of casualties soon followed us to the bureau of the hospital. In it was the death, at half-past nine o'clock, of " Jean Baptiste Bronneur, of the young guard, aged twenty-two." A youth who had not doubted either of the easy triumph of his Emperor, or of his own arrival at the rank of a marshal of France; who but yesterday contributed his utmost strength to the shouts of the Champ de Mai, and swelled the tide of self devotion at the field of Waterloo,—now stretched lifeless on his pallet, for the bad cause of that unworthy chief, who certainly had *he* seen the last moments, and listened to his own name on the dying lips of his devotee, would have been too much occupied with the means of saving the unwounded remnant of his own dishonoured days, to have spared other reflection than something about *sottise* or *dommage*. No associating principle of the most irresistible contrast, could more powerfully have recalled to our minds the flight and surrender of Napoleon Bonaparte, than the shrift and blessing of " Jean Baptiste Bronneur, de la jeune garde, agé vingt-deux'.' Yet did the phrenetic zeal for the emperor, in these poor creatures, seem to increase with their sufferings, and in the face of the full knowledge of his sacrifice and desertion of them. One man was pointed out, who had tossed his own amputated arm in the air, with a feeble shout of " vive l'Empereur." Another, at the moment of the preparations to take off his leg, declared, that there was something he knew of which would cure him on the spot, and save his limb and the operator's trouble. When asked to explain this wild remark, he said, " a sight of the Emperor!" The indispensable amputation did not save him; he died in the surgeon's hands; and his last words, stedfastly looking on his own blood, were, that he would cheerfully shed the last drop in his veins, for the great Napoleon!

A singularly wild and almost poetic fancy, was the form in which a third bore his testimony to his enthusiasm for his chief. He was undergoing, with matchless steadiness, the exquisite agony of the extraction of a ball from his side; and it happened to be the left. In the middle of the operation, he exclaimed, "an inch deeper, and you'll find the Emperor!" Had the Emperor merited such heroic devotion;—had he gloriously sacrificed himself in the field;—or had his cause been as great and good as it was profligate and wicked, there would have been no allaying reserve in the pathos and even sublimity of these singular scenes. But another reflection unseasonably intrudes, which at once renders the kind of scenes described repulsive and unsuitable. It is to be feared, that affections less amiable called forth these unexpected ebullitions. The vain, mortified, furious Frenchmen were preaching themselves at the moment, and not their idol. The latter was too well known, even in the effulgence of his power, ever to be personally loved; much more when the blindest of his worshippers could not but know that he had made a very safe and easy retreat in his own person; leaving them to *remember* him in all the horrors of the field and the hospital. But every vain Frenchman, identifying Napoleon's name with his *own* greatness, had committed himself so entirely, that to cease to cry out " *vive l'Empereur*," as long as breath or life lasted, was a thought not to be endured for a moment. A Frenchman, it is well known, lives for effect; and if circumstances only excite him enough, he will die for effect too. Wounded vanity and mortified pride will impel him to any thing; and accordingly a petulant and unyielding spirit, after defeat in battle, is the last thing to leave, if it ever leaves, the French soldier, or the French nation. Man and woman of them, tell the allied troops, who live as masters in their houses, in Paris itself, that *nonobstant,* they are not conquered ; while retrospectively talking of their own days of prosperity, in which the prostration of their most humiliated enemy never equalled their own, we hear of nothing but French *conquests,* and their *legitimate* fruits. A visit to theFrench requires a considerable stock of patience, among other requisites.

From the hospital of the Corderie, I was conducted by a guide, who was provided for me, into the impregnable citadel. It is considered as a master-piece of fortification The whole of the works, and the system of the garrison, were most obligingly explained to me by the governor, Colonel Crawfurd.

I had observed on the outside of the citadel, several parties of men dressed in shabby coarse red jackets, working at different sorts of hard labour, chained two and two by the legs with very heavy irons. The first party were attending two carts with a water cask on each ; and their march made a woeful rattling. They were the convicts, sent to Antwerp from all parts of the country, for a certain term of years, and many for life. Each party had a superintendant with it, and the description who are allowed to work out of doors, are the better behaved, and those whose time is near expiring. With an under keeper, my only guarantee, I went into their great prison, within the citadel; it consists of large wards, divided into stalls, like a long stable, placed head to head along the middle range, so as to leave the walls free on both sides to pass along. A man on the outside unlocked a huge iron grated door, and in a moment my conductor and I were among some hundreds of desperate criminals. This was worse than the French prisoners. I had often heard, that a visit to the felons of Newgate, is neither pleasant nor safe; but I could not help shuddering at the idea of being surrounded by foreign ruffians of all sorts. To my amazement, as we passsed along, the poor creatures, many of whom had left their stalls to go over to the opposite wall, about the length of their fetters, whenever they saw us, ran into their kennels, with a lamentable clanking, that we might not have to step over their chains; and one and all stood silent, and pulled off their caps to us as we passed. The governor told me, that this was not owing merely to there being an overseer with me; but that they would have done the same, had I been alone. I should not however have made the experiment.

The prison is kept well aired, and there are very few sick. The numbers are above 1000. Their submission probably results from the hoplessness of their situation, and the severe regime under which they are placed. To prevent even the thought of mutiny, loaded cannon are pointed to both sides of the prison. The two English regiments in the citadel, were the 37th and 25th.

The streets and walks were full of wounded officers, taking gentle exercise. To one very fine young man, an Irishman, I used the freedom of speaking. He was exceedingly emaciated and sadly lame; and he said he had received 24 sabre wounds. His servant was with him, watching and supporting his steps, with " 69th" marked on his cap; and as I was in quest of an officer of that regiment, I applied to this young man, who told me that the officer I wanted was in the same quarters with himself. I walked slowly home with him, and saw the object of my inquiry; he was quite recovered, and meant to proceed to Paris to join. They were very modest in their account of the battle, but naturally much pleased to hear that the country gave them due credit.

Much was said of the Highlanders in Antwerp. A gentleman whom I saw, had seen the wounded arrive. He himself had been recognised and spoken to by a poor wounded Highlander, which absolutely gave him a kind of consideration in the crowd. He felt prouder than if a prince had smiled upon him.

At Brussels, and wherever I went in the Netherlands, whenever the English troops were mentioned, whom they much admired, the natives always returned to the Scotch, with " Mais les Ecossais;" *They are good and kind as well as brave*; they are the only soldiers who become "*enfans de la famille*" in the houses in which they are billetted; they even carry the children, and do the domestic work. The favourite proverbial form of compliment was " Les Ecossais sont lions dans la battaille, et agneaux dans la maison :" *Lions in the field, and lambs in the house**. There was a competition among the inhabitants who should have them in their houses; and when they returned wounded, the same house they had left had its doors open, and the family went out some miles to meet " notre Ecossais," *our own Scotsman*. The people had many instances to relate of the generosity of these men; after the battle, many Highlanders, *themselves wounded*, were seen binding up the wounds of the French, and assisting them

---

* The Highland regiments are always called *Scotch*, and not Montagnards, or Highlanders, on the continent; which, unknown to the foreigners, is really their just appellation; as, it is well known, they are a mixture of Lowlanders and Highlanders.

with their arm. On the contrary, it is well known, that very few wounded Englishmen fell into the hands of the French, without being murdered in cold blood. There cannot be a better test of two nations, a better decision of the question on which the peace and happiness of mankind should depend.

With Mr. Annesly, the British consul, from whom and his interesting family I received much polite attention, I saw the docks constructed by Bonaparte, and the two first rate ships of war lying in the Scheldt. The river was full of English ships, and a number of the half-cured wounded were embarking for their homes. I went to the top of the tower of the great cathedral, nearly 400 feet high, and had a view at once of the whole of this vast town, with its citadel and fortifications. Its extent seemed at least equal to that of Edinburgh. The magnificent Scheldt winded under our eye, by Fort Lillo to Walcheren; and a rich, verdant, wooded, and grain-covered champaign, with many towns and villages, extended as far as the eye could reach, all around.

ANTWERP.

Antwerp itself is very grand and very ancient. It is most evidently Spanish, both in the style of its buildings, and costume of the lower order of its inhabitants. The hotels, or rather palaces of many of the Flemish noblesse who live in Antwerp, are in a style in the highest degree grand and sumptuous, resembling the first order of houses at the west end of Piccadilly. But in the same street, there is the continental incongruity of an intermixture of houses of the meanest rank, added to the total want of side pavement and sunk areas; the whole entirely destroying the impression to which the streets and squares of London, Dublin, and Edinburgh give rise, of their being peopled by the superior classes, without admixture of the vulgar.

The cathedral itself is one of the largest and most superb structures in the Netherlands; in the richest style of the florid Gothic. The towers are exquisitely ornamented, and elegantly light. The inside is also most splendid; and I observed with much interest the blanks carefully preserved for the divine pictures of Rubens, the *Ascent to the Cross*, the *Crucifixion*, and *Descent from the Cross*, which he had painted as the altar pieces of the cathedral of his native city; and which I afterwards saw actually taking down from the walls of the Louvre gallery, among the first in the progress of the great work of restitution.

CHAP. II.

BRUSSELS.

Road from Antwerp to Brussels—Place Royal—Park, with its buildings and ornaments—Preparations in Brussels for the battle—March of the troops—Of the Highland Regiments—Visit to Quatre Bras—Two English ladies—Retrograde movement of the British army—Alarms in Brussels—Wounded officer—Lady who had lost her husband—Alarm of fire at Antwerp—Field immediately after the battle—Robbery by a Prussian hussar—Irish officer and his young Belgian wife—Singular fortitude of the latter—Palace of Laken—Theatre

—King of the Netherlands present—A blacksmith necessary to disarm a Highland serjeant.

We passed through a country between Antwerp and Brussels, which seemed richer than any we had yet seen, and more varied in its beauty, from the undulations of its surface. Some places were of considerable acclivity; and on the ridge was generally an elegant country-seat, with gardens extending down to the road. Still the road, paved in the middle like our streets, was quite straight, and always inclosed with a row of high trees on each side. The crops were in many places reaping; two or three men cut with a short scythe (the *Heinault*) in one hand, and a kind of hook in the other, to gather the corn, and to serve the purpose of holding it tight till the other instrument strikes it. They seem to get on quickly enough in this manner; and here, as in Holland, much field labour was going forward, although it was Sunday.

We passed through the town of Mechline; so famous for its lace, and also for its cathedral.

Sunday is a kind of market day in the Flemish towns; the shops are all open; and, before and after the church service, the peasantry are buying cloth, provisions, and other articles.

On entering Brussels, the same busy scene presented itself; a tenfold proportion to that at Mechline.

I went with a guide out of the Namur gate, and about half a mile in the suburbs, found the house of a relation of my own and his wife for some time resident at Brussels.

Our way led us to cross a part of the splendid new town of this capital of the Netherlands. On our way, it was striking to see on many doors, written in chalk, 1, 2, or 3 blessés. This was probably for the convenience of the medical men. Sometimes it was " 2 officiers blessés*," and on one door I read " 2 Anglois, and 2 Ecossais blessés†." This was nearer and

---

* Two officers wounded.

† Two English, and two Scotch wounded.

nearer Waterloo, and I felt a great veneration for these chalked doors.

On entering the great square, or Place Royal, I was arrested in amazement by its magnificence. It seems about the size of the principal squares of London or Edinburgh, without an enclosed garden in the center. The houses are all in the style of the most elegant houses in Piccadilly; and built of cream-coloured brick, but with more of stone ornaments and statuary. They are on an uniform and regular plan, with a beautiful church of Grecian architecture in the center of one side. The streets enter by the middle of the sides, and the corners are filled up by beautiful arcades or porticos, surmounted by statues, warlike trophies, &c. in pure white marble. I have seen nothing which gave me more the impression of a square of palaces than this noble *place*. The streets run out from the square, and inclose what is called the park or public walk. These houses, arranged in rows at least half a mile long, are in the same style of magnificence; interrupted here and there, in their uniformity, by a sumptuous public building, with noble porticos, and rails; and a richness of white ornament in statuary on the creamcoloured brick, which has really a royal appearance. The park is beautifully planted, and traversed by walks in such a manner, that a magnificent palace, seems to form a vista to each; and every alley abounds in copies in marble from the finest statues, very tastefully disposed. I have no where seen any thing so completely elegant and grand as this new town of Brussels, with the exception of the Place de Louis XV. at Paris, with its magnificent vistas. The rest of the town is like Antwerp, only much inferior. Very Spanish is the appearance of the older houses; and the women, as in Antwerp, wear the Spanish veil.

So recently after the great day, the battle was, in Brussels, perhaps still more than in Antwerp, as so much nearer the scene, the constant and deeply interesting subject of conversation. To my friend and his lady, who had been in Brussels at the time, and had endured all the alarms and horrors, and run all the risks of that unparalleled period, it was naturally an inexhaustible subject. They had seen the ravages of the plague in Malta, and come through many other difficulties. But all was forgotten in the scenes which they witnessed upon the late tremendous occasion. There is no way of giving a more lively account of these, than shortly relating, as they recounted it to me, their own share in the memorable days of June.

It is well known, that the news of the French having attacked the Prussians at Charleroi, on the 15th, reached the Duke of Wellington when at a ball at the Duke of Richmond's, and produced his prompt departure for the rendezvous of the British army, at Quatre Bras. The inhabitants of Brussels were roused from their slumbers in the silence of the night, by the drums and bugles of alarm; and poured out of their houses to increase the confusion. My friend among the rest immediately repaired to the Place Royal, where, and in the park, unagitated by alarm, our brave troops were making their preparations, and taking their places with all the composure of an ordinary parade. The artillery, the cavalry, the waggon train, were all in perfect order in the park; and setting out with alacrity to meet the enemy. The sun was rising when the march began: every regiment went off with three cheers, in the midst of the inhabitants, who had crowded every spot where they could get a last look of them, and follow them with their blessings and prayers. My friend was naturally most affected with, and loved most to recount, the steady, serious, business-like march of the Highland regiments, who were about to justify, and exceed the utmost that has been said and expected of them in the Netherlands. " God protect the brave Scotch;" " God cover the heads of our gallant friends," were often repeated as they passed along; and many a flower was thrown from many a fair hand into their ranks. In three hours, the Place Royal and the Park, were empty and silent; and the inhabitants retired to their houses in a state of anxiety which needs no description.

Very early next morning, my friend set out for Quatre Bras, moved by a most natural sympathy, having seen the regiment in which he had once served, pass through for the scene of action.

He was much affected by meeting on the road, on their way back from the sad field, two English ladies on horseback, unattended, in agonies of grief and despair, which spoke too plainly their cause. He saw the memorable scene of the short but brilliant affair of Quatre Bras ; an affair, which although forming really a part of Waterloo, has its own separate merits of the highest rank. Let it never be forgotten, that here, 9000 of the Guards and Highlanders, and some other gallant regiments, with about 4000 Brunswick troops and Belgians, without cavalry or artillery, actually drove back Marshal Ney, at the head of 50,000 men, and bivouacked for the night on the enemy's first position. Our loss was immense. The Highland garb was particularly conspicuous among the slain. These brave men, cheered in the morning by their admiring friends, when marching out of Brussels, lay dead absolutely in ranks. The striking circumstance is noticed in a very distinct account of the campaign, published in Paris by a French officer, who was himself in the whole of it; to which I shall in the sequel, make frequent references *.

---

* " The road, and skirts of the wood, were concealed " by heaps of dead, of which the greater part were Scotch. " Their costume, which consists of a kind of short wrap- " ping coat, *(une jacquette plissée)*, made of a sort of brown " stuff interspersed with stripes of blue, and which, hard- " ly reaching so low as the knee, leaves a part of the limb " uncovered, singularly attracted the attention of the " French soldiers, who gave them the name of *sans cu-* " *lottes.*"

Relation par une Temoin Oculaire.

In returning, my friend was astonished on looking round, to see the English troops in full retreat; that admirable movement, which enabled Lord Wellington to concentrate his whole force at Waterloo, about eight miles in rear of Quatre Bras. He was soon overtaken, and his gig could not get on an inch farther; the road was completely choaked up. He thought of leaving it, and taking to the fields; but finding that he got on at least at the pace of the retreating army, he kept his seat, and arrived safe on the Saturday night at Brussels. It thundered and lightened to such a degree, that the road seemed in one blaze. To this was added successive reports spread in Brussels, that the French had carried all before them, and were just at the gates, to massacre, plunder, and burn. About mid-day on the Saturday, the first of the panic-struck Prussians from Charleroi and Sombref, began to crowd in hundreds to Brussels. They were at first taken for French; but when they were known, their flight and panic gave even greater alarm. Although at least 15 miles from a Frenchman, the horsemen galloped, cutting their horses with their sabres, the infantry ran, and the whole passed on the road under my friend's window; at which his lady sat in indescribable anxiety and terror. Nobody would admit the flying Prussians; the gate Namur, and all the entrances to the town, were closed; and many English gentlemen were seen urging the Prussians to return to their colours. These fugitives lay down in crowds, on the pavements of the suburbs, and on the Boulevards under the walls.

Towards the afternoon, the wounded English of Quatre Bras began to arrive; and instead of shutting the gates, the town poured out to meet them, and each family was anxious to find if their own inmate was among them. For the Highlanders they could not do too much; and even the ladies attended them and dressed their wounds.—Sunday came, and the battle about nine miles off began to roar. It was described by the inhabitants of Brussels, as one uninterrupted peal of thunder in their ears for eight hours.

> "Then great events were in the gale,
> "And each hour brought a varying tale."

But the fears of the inhabitants always made the French successful.—What then must they have felt, when the English baggage past through Brussels, and crowded the road to Antwerp. No wonder that the rumour was *then* believed, that the French had gained a complete victory. The entire population were now to fly; a pretty strong piece of evidence of no great attachment to the French. *Nous sommes perdus, Nous sommes perdus* *, was the only cry to be heard among the inhabitants. My friend resolved on flight on his lady's account, and had the extraordinary fortune to get to Mechline, about 15 miles, unhurt. They got a place in the track-boat on the canal; and being close to the road, saw all its horrors. When horses fell, the waggon wheels crushed the

* We are lost.

rider: baggage was thrown off and carried away by the peasants to be cut open and plundered. Great sums of money were in this way lost, and clothes, and other property spread over the fields. An English officer, who had lost a foot, and was carried on his servant's back, came and begged to be taken into the boat. He was known to my friend, who, although the passengers, intent on self-preservation opposed it, by absolute force obtained his admission. At Mechline they found it very difficult to get into a house; and the difficulty was increased, when the people were told that the lady was ill. Expecting to become an hospital, one house refused them admittance; but they succeeded in another. Most providentially they procured a voiture to Antwerp next day. On their arrival there, they heard an altercation between their coachman and a woman on the top, whom he had taken up, and would not let down till she paid a franc. They found this poor *detenue* to be the widow, newly so made, of a soldier killed at Quatre Bras; and the mother of a child which she had the day before seen crushed to death by a waggon wheel! Many of the wounded were travelling the same road; some had lost a hand or an arm; thousands were on foot; and all sorts of carriages and horses crowded the road and increased the danger. The scene was beyond description horrible; but a feeling of terror and self-preservation actually much diminished the concern for the sufferers. This is very common in the horrors of war.—The persons crushed in the flight to Antwerp, were just thrown into the ditches; and all this was witnessed by my friend and his wife. The confusion was dreadful, yet no one had seen a single Frenchman.

When my friends arrived at Antwerp, the first sight they saw was heart-rending. An officer's lady had just learned that her husband's head had been shot off at Quatre Bras. The poor lady was running about the market-place, hysterical and delirious, with a little boy crying and running after her. "My husband is not dead, he is just coming; his head is not shot off." The people did all they could to console her when they saw her condition, and learned what she said.—Hardly had they sat down in Antwerp, when an alarm was spread which added to their terrors. A servant of the hotel ran into their room almost breathless, calling "feu, feu, feu!" "Where is the fire?"—"O, it is in a vessel on the canal, in the midst of several powder ships, and the whole town will share the fate of Leyden." To their great relief, they were soon informed that the fire was got under.

In the course of the Monday, the news of the defeat of the French arrived; and on Tuesday my friend and his wife returned to Brussels. On the Wednesday he went out again to see the field of Waterloo. His account of it is dreadful. The first thing which struck him at a distance, was the quantity of caps and hats strewed on the ground. It appeared as if the field had been covered with crows. When he came to the spot, the sight was truly shocking. At first there was a prodigious preponderance of British slain, which looked very ill; but more in advance, the revenge made itself dreadfully marked; ten French lay dead for one British. The field was so much covered with blood, that it appeared as if it had been completely flooded with it; dead horses seemed innumerable,— and the peasantry employed in burying the dead, generally stript the bodies first. Of course these people got a vast booty, when they ventured out of the neighbouring wood after the battle; many of them made some hundred pounds. A great quantity of cap plates, cuirasses, &c. were taken by them and sold as relics.

The scene was for a week exposed to another danger. The Prussian dragoons had left stragglers, who robbed many persons on the field. I saw an inhabitant of Brussels who, with three others, was surveying the field on the Thursday after the battle, and had got upon the road about a quarter of a mile beyond Belle Alliance, when round a rising ground galloped a Prussian hussar with drawn sabre, who was amongst them in an instant:—" Your watches, your money, or I will cut you down."

The marauder's commands were obeyed; and when the four people returned to the village of Mount St. John, they related their maladventure to *four* of our own countrymen, who confessed that they too had allowed this fortunate hussar to serve them in the same manner. I do not think that *every four* Englishmen would have been robbed by one man, however completely armed or mounted.

I had the good fortune to travel from Brussels to Paris, with a young Irish officer and his wife, an Antwerp lady of only sixteen; of great beauty, and matchless innocence and *naiveté*. The husband was in the battle of Quatre Bras, as well as of Waterloo, and to him I owe much of my minutest and most interesting information.

An anecdote of his fair Belgian, which he justly took some pride in relating, will further serve to give an idea of the kind of scenes then occurring, the horrors and the dangers of which it is difficult to describe.

He was living in cantonments at Nivelles, his wife with him. The unexpected advance of the French called him off on a moment's notice to Quatre Bras; but he left with his wife his servant, one horse, and the family baggage which was packed upon a large ass. Retreat at the time was not anticipated, but being suddenly ordered on the Saturday morning, he contrived to get a message to his wife to make the best of her way, attended by the servant and baggage, to Brussels. The servant, a foreigner, had availed himself of the opportunity to take leave of both master and mistress, and made off with the horse, leaving the helpless young lady alone with the baggage ass. With a firmness becoming the wife of a British officer, she boldly commenced on foot *her own* retreat of 25 miles, leading the baggage ass by the bridle, and carefully preserving the baggage. No violence was dared by any one to so innocent a pilgrim, but no one could afford to assist her. She was soon in the midst of the columns of the retreating British army, and much retarded and endangered by the artillery; her fatigue was great; it rained in waterspouts, and the thunder and lightning were dreadful in the extreme. She continued to advance, and got upon the great road from Charleroi to Brussels at Waterloo, when the army on the Saturday evening were taking up their line for the awful conflict. In so extensive a field, and among 80,000 men, it was in vain to seek her husband; she knew that the sight of her *there*, would only have embarrassed and distressed him; she kept slowly advancing to Brussels all the Saturday night; the road choaked with all sorts of conveyances, waggons, and horses; multitudes of native fugitives on the road, and flying into the great wood; and many of the wounded working their painful way, dropping every step, and breathing their last; every few steps lay a corpse, or a limb; particularly, she said, *severed hands;* many persons were actually killed by others, if by chance they stood in the way of their endeavours to save themselves. And to add to the horrors, the rain continued unabated, and the thunder and lightning still raged as if the heavens were torn to pieces. Full twelve miles further in the night this young woman marched, up to her knees in mud, her boots worn entirely off, so that she was barefooted; but still unhurt, she led her ass; and although thousands lost their baggage, and many their lives, she calmly entered Brussels in the morning in safety, self, ass, bag and baggage, without the loss of an article. In a few hours after her arrival, commenced the cannon's roar of the tremendous Sunday; exposed to which, for ten hours, she knew her husband to be; and after a day and night of agony, she was rewarded by finding herself in her husband's arms, he unhurt, and she nothing the worse, on the Monday. The officer told me the tale himself, with tears in his eyes. With a slight Irish accent, he called her his " dare little woman," and said she became more valuable to him every day. I never saw a more elegant gentleman-like young man; and assuredly his pretty Belgian seemed almost to adore him. It gave additional value to the foregoing anecdote, that I had it from the actors in the scene described. When I remarked that it was quite in the spirit of Elizabeth of Siberia, the lady exclaimed, " Ah ! ma mère dit la même chose * !"

We paid a visit to the beautiful palace of La en, in the vicinity ; from which Bonaparte had dated the proclamations to the Belgians, taken in his baggage. It is a superb house, something like the Register Office of Edinburgh, with the same kind of dome ; but having a much more elegant appearance, from its fine ornaments in statuary. It is situated on the summit of a beautiful sloping ground, all of which is laid out with great taste in the manner of English landscape gardening. A Tivoli temple adorns the grounds, very inferior indeed, in both size and correct architecture, to St. Bernard's well, near Edinburgh, which is certainly one of the most perfect buildings of the kind out of Italy. The apartments in the palace are in high style and taste, though far inferior in magnificence to those of the palace at Amsterdam ; but in convenience and elegance, I think they have a decided advantage. Laken,

* My mother made the same remark.

as well as Amsterdam, was furnished from Paris by Bonaparte. His favourite apartments are shewn, as a kind of trophies by the servants of the present royal owner; his bed-room, and above all, his bath. A Dutch young lady, who was of our party, was persuaded to pull the gold tassel of the bath bell which Napoleon must often have handled; but with great horror, and perfect gravity, immediately rubbed her hand to wipe off the pollution.

We saw the grand museum, to which purpose the ancient palace of the Spanish government of this country is converted; the library appears very good, and the paintings are numerous, and by the first masters of nearly all the schools. We likewise saw a private collection, belonging to an old gentleman, and were much pleased with it. The proprietor, M. Bourtine, went through the rooms with us himself. We went to the theatre, which is much superior to that of Antwerp; and saw part of a French comedy. The King, who had just arrived from Holland, was present, which gave us an opportunity of observing how he was received by his new subjects. Nothing could be more loyal and flattering than their reception of him; and many allusions were made to the brave Prince and his glorious wound: A most blessed wound for the House of Orange.

I delivered a collection of numbers of the Transactions of the Royal Society of Edinburgh, to Mr. Van Mons, a Brussels *sçavan*. Even his conversation was all of Waterloo, and, that interminable theme, the Scotch regiments. One Highland sergeant, formerly billeted in Mr. Van Mons' house, came back, with the basket hilt of his sword so bruised, that he could not get his hand out of it, till relieved by a blacksmith! He made very light of his wounds, and only hoped soon to be " at the enemy again." There was no *disarming* him without the aid of a blacksmith!

In crossing the grand market place of Brussels from Mr. Van Mons' house, I was much surprised to see women riding after the fashion of the other sex. One was sitting on a tall horse, haranguing a crowd as a mountebank doctress, attended by a man who beat a drum. Her fluency of speech was amazing.

Indeed I saw women frequently addressing the public in long speeches, recommending their wares, or glossing over their impositions.

A foolish report was current in Brussels, that the Netherlands were to be exchanged by Holland with England for Hanover. The arrangement however, seemed to give very general satisfaction. Nothing can exceed the attachment of the Flemings in general to the English, and the change of sentiment of the former friends of France *since* the battle. All benefit from France is now at an end, and loyalty has become the best policy. It will much improve as public affairs get better arranged. The men are every where training to arms for the House of Orange, who have risen immensely in public esteem since the Prince's wound.

I learned from my friends, that they had soon found out my wounded relation in the Guards, formerly mentioned, who told them that he was shot in the famous wood at Quatre

Bras; and when carried to the rear had recollection enough to be sensible that three attempts were made by the enemy's tirailleurs to take his life. He spent the night in a cottage, which was soon filled with the wounded; several of whom died before the morning. Fortunately for him, the enemy's troops did not move early next day; and having set off some hours before the retreat, he passed Waterloo without being overtaken. He was held upon his horse by his servant, and was repeatedly laid down on the road-side, exhausted with pain and loss of blood. Had the enemy driven back the British, it is evident, he must have remained in their hands.

He has himself, since I have seen him, confirmed the above account.

CHAP. III.

VISIT TO THE FIELD.

Forest of Soignè—Village of Waterloo—Station of Lord Wellington—Description of the field—Discouraging bivouac—Spirit of an Irish officer—Numbers of the two armies—Exclamation of Bonaparte—Three first attacks—Effect of their failure on Napoleon—Infantry attacks, a kind of breathing to the British troops—Impatience of the British troops to be led on—Their constancy and firmness—Farm house of La Haye Sainte—Sir William De Lancey—Colonel Miller, and Captain Curzon—Horror of the field the day after

VISIT TO THE FIELD. 53

the battle—*Wreck yet remaining, leaves of books and letters*—*Chivalrous conduct of the Prince of Orange*—*Anecdote of a nameless Regiment of volunteer light horse*—*12th light Dragoons, young officer of that regiment who fell*—*Brigade of 30th, and another regiment*—*Several anecdotes*—*69th regiment*—*Hougoumont and the guards*—*Hovel of Belle Alliance, interesting visit to*—*Country over which the enemy fled*—*Admirable manœuvre of the 52d and 71st regiments*—*Visit to the station of Napoleon*—*Lacoste the farmer*—*Answer of Napoleon to message about an English battery*—*His compliments to the British troops*—*His interview with a British officer*—*Account by a French officer, of his behaviour*—*Appearance of the Prussians*—*Final effort of Napoleon*—*Its defeat by the Highlanders and Scots Greys*—CHARGE BY THE WHOLE BRITISH ARMY—*Beautiful compliment from the Prussian to the British cavalry*—*French officer's account of the route of the French Army*—*Flight of Napoleon*—*Contrast of the conduct of Frederick the Great*—*Megret's remark on the death of Charles the XII.—Specimen of the spoil of a poor Highlander—Anecdote of a peasant woman on the field.*

With that conflict of feelings, which the expectation of soon seeing the scene of such a battle as Waterloo naturally occasioned, our party, consisting of three, was in readiness by six in the morning, on the 31st of July.—When we had mounted our carriage, we called to the postillion—" *Waterloo!*"—" Oui, Monsieur L'Anglais," he answered, with a smack of his whip, and an emphasis, which shewed that he felt, that, conducting Englishmen *there*, was conducting them to their own proper domain. There had been rain during the night, and the morning was gloomy; having, as we were told, the same appearance as that of the 18th of June; of course we would not have exchanged it for the brightest sunshine. The ground would be wet,—but so it was on the day of the battle; and further, in point of time, we should just arrive about the hour it commenced.

After driving three or four miles, we entered the aweful forest of Soigné. It covers an immense extent of country from east to west, but is only about six or seven miles broad, where the road runs through it to Waterloo.

The impressions of an Englishman on entering this wood, are much enhanced by the knowledge of the fact that it was the great source of supply of ship-timber for Napoleon's naval schemes at Antwerp, and already had built several ships of the line. The same forest which was intended to furnish the means of her humiliation protected the rear of her victorious army, on the day, when, *single handed*, England at one blow, destroyed the power of her destroyer for ever.

Every foot of the road was interesting as it held its very straight course through the wood. We contrasted the gloomy quiet of our journey,—a few peasants going to their early labour,—with its accumulated horrors on the day of the retreat of the baggage and wounded of the army; the multitudes who dropt and died; the numbers who were crushed to death;

the hurry, the alarm, the confusion ; the cries, and shrieks, and groans of that dreadful scene; and the interesting unprotected " *Elizabeth*," formerly described, steadily and safely, by a miracle, leading her gallant husband's baggage ass in the middle of it. Our carriage kept the paved chaussé, or centre of the way; the two sides, of about 15 feet wide each, being deep and muddy, as they were on the great occasion. The whole breadth of the road might be 40 or 50 feet. The trees which bounded it on each side were tall, and kept trimmed like a very high hedge or screen ; beyond them immediately commenced the thick wood, in all the irregularity of nature. Here the wounded had crawled, and died in great numbers ; much baggage had been plundered ; and the whole population of the country had fled for safety.

Our postilion pointed out the little mounds where men and horses had been interred ; they were apparent every hundred yards. The septure had been hurried and imperfect, especially of the horses ; occasional hoofs, and even limbs, shewing themselves. Often bayonet scabbards stuck out; and caps, shoes, and pieces of cloth, scarcely in the gloom distinguishable from the mud in which they lay, gave indication of the spots where many a soldier after bleeding in the field, and toiling along the road to expected aid and comfort, had sunk to rise no more; unassisted, almost unpitied, by the self-engaged sufferers who saw him fall. Some rain fell as we were bestowing a passing survey upon these affecting monuments of the brave, in a situation the most dismal we had ever beheld.

Waterloo's village, and small neat church with its brick built dome, was now in our view, situated in a sinuosity of the wood evidently cleared for it. The road was now quite out of the forest; which, however, blackened the whole region to east and west as far as the eye could reach. In this poor hamlet, which history is to name with veneration as long as time endures, the peasants have been at pains to preserve the chalking on the doors; on which we recognised the well-known names of celebrated officers, or the several departments at head-quarters.

We were immediately surrounded by the people, offering for sale, with great importunity, relics of the field; particularly the eagles which the French soldiers wore as cap plates. A few cuirasses, both the back and the breast pieces, were likewise held up to us, as well as sabres, bayonets, and other spoil.

We drove a mile forward to the still smaller hamlet of Mount St. John, by a gradual ascent of the road; to right and left of which, the British army bivouacked on the eve of the battle; having advanced over the high ground in the morning to the southern slope facing the enemy, on fair open ground, without an advantage, to decide the fate of the world.

Mount St. John, it will be seen by the annexed Plan, is quite behind the British line; and had its name given by Bonaparte to what was properly the farm house of La Haye Sainte, which he did succeed in carrying; but certainly he never was so far advanced as Mount St. John; indeed he never did, for more than a few minutes at any time, succeed in penetrating the English line.

We left our carriage at Mount St. John, and walked on to the field with nervous anticipation. To the right and left were the multiplied marks of the artillery wheels; as rivalling " lightning's course in ruin and in speed" they had careered to their station in the memorable line. Whole tracks were marked by the feet of the cavalry, often fetlock deep in the mud. The last homes of the brave began to appear, with the larger tumuli of their horses, more frequent as we approached the scene of contest. Keeping still the great road, we came, directed by our plan, to a tree which formed the precise centre of the British line; the well chosen station of the Duke of Wellington, when not occasionally visiting other parts of the position to confirm the unflinching spirit of his gallant comrades. It commanded a full view of the intermediate plain, and the whole of the enemy's vast force upon the adverse slope and country beyond it, with every movement made or threatened him.

Nothing is more false than the French apology, (added to their never-failing pretence of being overpowered by numbers), that the British position was naturally strong, and carefully fortified. *Unentrenched* stood the British army, along its whole position, on a slope so gentle, that a coach driving up, would not slacken pace; and to the ridge of which the French cavalry found no difficulty of galloping at full speed to the very bayonets of their opponents, who threw themselves into squares, their only entrenchments, to receive them. It was, to use a favourite English phrase, just the place for " *a fair set to ; a clear field and no favour.*"

We had the good fortune to meet with a very intelligent English officer, who had been in the action, and who had that day paid his first visit to the field, after recovering of his wound.

VISIT TO THE FIELD. 61

From Lord Wellington's station, we stood and gazed on the whole scene; not daring to break silence for some minutes. And deep was now the silence of the vast sepulchre of 20,000 men, contrasted with the roar and the carnage of the battle. The gloomy weather still lasted; and was valued by us, as peculiarly suitable to the scene we were contemplating. The imagination is incalculably advanced, by seeing the scene of a memorable battle. The actors being generally familiar to us, we can easily people the field with them; and become thereby actually present, in conception, at the moment of the event. Indeed, so very simple is the field of Waterloo, that a conception of very ordinary power may quite take it in from description alone. Although here and there, varied by inequalities and undulations, it will serve all ordinary popular purposes, to say, that at the distance from each other of about a mile, the contending armies occupied parallel high grounds, sloping with almost equadeclivity, to a plain of about half a mile broad which intervened.

The English line, or rather two lines, extended about a mile and a half. The French masses something more than two miles.

The Brussels road ran at right angles through both armies; forming the centre of each. On this road, in one line, are the villages of Waterloo, and Mount St. John, and the farm houses of La Haye Sainte, and La Belle Alliance; and the only other place which requires to be referred to, is the memorable Chateau of Hougomont, advanced a short way in front of nearly the right of the British position. The road from Brussels to Nivelles, which branches off at Waterloo from the great road already described, passed the right of the army; which last being thrown back into a curve, crossed the angle formed by the two roads, like the scale of a quadrant. A number of smaller roads and foot-paths intersected the field in all directions, none of them of any importance in the affair, excepting always those roads, which admitted the brave Prussians to their share of the glory of the deliverance of the world.

The whole will at once be illustrated, by glancing at the Plan annexed to this volume.

The night before the battle, the troops lay down, already drenched with the heavy rain, on the deep mud of the ground. Every one must have remarked, that by a singular fatality, our brave army have often had very unfavourable weather for their greater exploits. The country had been quite dry till the movement of the troops from their cantonments; on the 17th, the rain and thunder and lightning continued almost without intermission, till the morning of Waterloo, when it ceased; and the weather became fine again. Fortunately, there was too much excitement of spirit, for this physical inconvenience to be much felt, either at the time or afterwards. The men were fresh from cantonments; and their toil, though severe, was short. Never did British army take the field in finer condition. The cavalry especially felt the benefit of fighting, before losing the effects of their superior keeping, by the toils and privations of a campaign. The Irish officer, formerly mentioned as my travelling companion to Paris, recounted the effect of the wet bivouac on himself, in a manner which gives a striking view of the high feeling of the men who sustain in the field the honour of our country. When he got up about six o'clock in the morning, he could not stand with a violent shivering; but fell down in the mud again. He made several efforts, but in vain. Without dreaming, when he recounted the circumstance, of an inference favourable to himself, which he was not aware that I was drawing, he described his feelings to have been perfect agony, *arising from the dread that he should not be able to do his duty.* An hour or two, and a little brandy revived him; and when he found he could stand, his relief of mind amounted to the most exquisite joy he ever felt in his life. Yet 130,000 ferocious enemies were full in his view,—he distinctly heard the shout of " vive l'Empereur," the signal for the tremendous onset;

death was coming on in its most threatening aspect,—in the gloom of the morning, the vast, broad, and deep masses of the enemy, with their mighty reserves yet further and further back till they seemed to meet the horizon, appeared, as he expressed himself, as if the forest of Soignè had changed its situation. Yet, did this fearless youth feel his heart leap for joy when he found himself able, for the honour of Ireland, *to stand up* to the coming storm! On higher principle yet than the Oneida chief,

"Fearing but the shame of fear."

I heard in Paris, an officer of the 95th, with the same manly absence of self-gratulation, give nearly the same account of his own trials on the memorable dawn of Waterloo. Who can wonder at the virtue with which the entire day was sustained, when such were the feelings with which the battle was waited for, and begun.

When cooking their breakfasts, the troops were called to desist, by the spirit-stirring preparative from the aids-du-camp passing at full gallop—" Stand to your arms, the French are moving." As we stood on our commanding spot, the first thought was most naturally the numbers respectively of the contending forces. The British were stated by Bonaparte himself at 80,000, and certainly they have never been made out to have been more. Of these not more than 30,000 were actually British; the rest, Germans, Belgians, and Dutch.

The French army certainly were 130,000, making the enormous balance in their favour of 50,000 men; and, be it never forgotten, *all French;* and the best troops of France. Marshal Ney, in his justification to the Duke of Otranto, calls them, " that fine and numerous army;" a character at once decisive of the question, when it is considered what that army must have been which a French marshal would think of so characterising. But, " The *Relation,*" published in Paris by a French officer, formerly referred to, states in plain terms, without intending to diminish, and certainly with the reverse of interest to exaggerate, that the French army which attacked the Duke of Wellington, was 120,000 strong. His testimony is the more satisfactory as to the absolute numbers of the French, that, with true national feeling, in his ignorance of the truth, he ludicrously overrates the British force; and brings fresh masses *out of the wood of Soignè*, just as they were needed; " pour ecrasser par les nombres *" the *overwhelmed* columns of the French. In truth the British army were a mile and a half from the utmost skirts of the wood, and never had one man within it: And so far from being crushed or overlaid, the masses, and of the French guard too, were often routed by the bold dash of an almost incredibly small proportion of their numbers; nay sometimes, as will afterwards be told, of the Highlanders and Scots Greys, and it happened in many other parts of the

* To crush by numbers.

field besides, by the prodigies of nearly isolated, individual valour.

Bonaparte knew the number of his already devoted adversaries well; and with his usual presumption expressed great astonishment to see their undismayed front on *that* side of the forest. His fear was that they would escape him in the night, and he exclaimed, on first seeing their order of battle, with the dawn—" Ah ! je les tiens donc, ces Anglois* !"

The battle, it is well known, commenced by the almost simultaneous advance (and we distinctly saw their course) of three entire *corps d'armee* on the right, left, and center of the British line. The attack on the right had for its first object the carrying of the post of Hougomont, the key of the position; in possession of which, the French could have turned the British right. That column had shortest way to move; and, under king Jerome, it was there the cannon and musketry first began. As admitted by " The *Relation*," fresh reinforcements were

---

* Ah, I have them then, these English !

VISIT TO THE FIELD. 69

sent to this scene of carnage repeatedly to no purpose. The utmost success of probably 30,000 men, was obliging the light companies of the 1st, 2d, and 3d foot guards, under the command of Lord Saltoun, to take refuge *within* the post, instead of defending the small wood on the outside of it. The post itself was never occupied for a moment. The guards kept it, in spite of grape, and musketry, and balls, and shells; and in spite too of the partial success of the enemy to set it on fire, because they could not gain possession of it; till its brave defenders issued from it, in the hour of vengeance, when the victory was decided.

The corps d'armee destined to attack the left, (the 6th,) soon arrived at the first attack in that quarter, about the center of the British left wing, but were calmly received and repulsed, first by the admirably served artillery, and then by the 42d, 79th, and 92d Highlanders, and some other equally gallant regiments, under the lamented Sir Thomas Picton. The whole slope was in our view.

Nothing could be more tremendous than the mode of attack; it was always headed by artillery, which discharged showers of iron grape shot, each bullet larger than a walnut*. It was a battle, on the part of the French, of cavalry and cannon, both equipped as if by magic, and much more formidable than had ever been known, in the French armies even, to take the field. " L'artillerie," says " The *Relation*," " se porta en avant, sur *toute* la ligne, et les colonnes la suivirent†." Heading these columns were the iron-cased cuirassiers, in as complete mail, breast and back, as in the days of that defensive armour; upon which the musket balls were heard to ring as they glanced off without injuring, or even stunning the wearer. These *men at arms*, had immense infantry columns of support at their backs. By looking at the Plan, it will be seen that a stunted hedge bounded each side of a narrow cross road, which ran along the whole of the

* Some of these dreadful balls we found on the field.

† The artillery advanced *in front* along the whole line; and the columns followed.

British left wing, joining the great road near the Duke of Wellington's tree already mentioned. In the hedge there were a number of gaps, which had been made to serve as a kind of embrazures for the line of the British cannon of the left wing, and a trifling bank only here and there two or three feet high, on which the hedge grew, and in which apertures for the guns were cut where necessary, was the only thing resembling shelter which any portion of our artillery enjoyed;—and may have given occasion to the author of " The *Relation*" to speak of appearances of fresh earth turned up in the British position. But, as will appear in the sequel, the Greys found no difficulty in brushing through the hedge and leaping over the works, as a nearer road than round their flank, to get at the enemy. When the cannon and infantry had staggered the masses of the enemy, and somewhat calmed their inordinate fury; round the extremity of the cross road, full on their flank, wheeled, like a whirlwind, the unlooked-for First Dragoons, Scots Greys, and Enniskillens

In vain the iron cases,—the cuirassiers were " bouleversés et culbutes *," (in the words of " The *Relation*,") their cannon was deserted and taken; and the columns of infantry were thrown into such confusion, that they had just time to get beyond the range of the prudent pursuit of their adversaries, whose warfare *yet* was defensive. The dragoons, Highlanders, and other infantry, with their captured cannon and eagles, calmly returned to their place in position, to await the next advance of the enemy.

If our present ground had the well fought *round* now faintly described in full view; so had Napoleon's station, about a mile along the road from where we stood. With the poor farmer Lacoste pinioned on horseback beside him, stood the Emperor; unable to conceal his astonishment at the recoil and almost flight of his finest troops; and constrained, in spite of

* There is no translating these expressive words when describing the effect of a charge of cavalry. Boyer's dictionary renders the first *to turn topsy turvy*, and the second *to throw head over heels.*

him, repeatedly to mutter compliments to the spirit, rapidity, and steadiness of the British cavalry. "These English fight admirably," said he to Soult, "but they *must* give way." "No, they prefer being cut to pieces," was the answer of one who knew *something* of them. The grey horses especially struck him, and he often repeated, " quelles superbes troupes."

The centre attack was most of this time in full activity, and overwhelming efforts were making to gain the farm house of La Haye Sainte, advanced two or three hundred yards from the British position. Here Fortune bestowed one melancholy smile on Napoleon's arms. No moment even of temporary success was theirs *in* the line; but they did establish themselves, *with twenty to one*, in the post of La Haye Sainte, in consequence, as the Duke of Wellington's account testifies, of the unexpected failure of the ammunition of a detachment of the German legion, to which its defence was committed; a failure which, from the position and great strength of the enemy, it was at the time considered impossible to supply. This very limited, and, as it turned out *bootless*, success of the enemy, it appears is matter of much self-reproach to the commander in chief. He has often been heard to use very hard words, when speaking of what he calls his own want of presence of mind on the occasion. It was impossible to send ammunition in by the gates at the two sides of the farm yard, but it might have approached the *back* of the house, under cover of the British fire, and been handed in by an aperture made on purpose.

Considering what the general on such a day had to think of, it will not be thought surprising, that with all his commanding influence, the Duke of Wellington has not succeeded in inducing any of his auditors to join in his accusation.

He has one comfort; the post, when carried with immense loss, did no good to the captors. It neutralised a large force; and never for a moment shook the British centre.

The three attacks now described, we were told, might serve as a fair specimen of the reiterated war during the entire day. From eleven in the morning till seven at night, it consisted of a succession of such attacks, with unabated fury, and increasing force; and often with a boldness and deadly effect, which perplexed our soldiers, and put their matchless firmness to the utmost trial. It may be believed, that every fresh onset swept away multitudes of our infantry; still the survivors gave not an inch of the ground, but made good the lines and firm the squares. No men in Europe could have endured as they did: Again and again the enemy's cannon and cavalry rebounded as it were from their " adamantine front," dismayed and scattered. These were the *breathing* times of our heroes! Line was with admirable alacrity formed for a greater breadth of fire than the squares afforded, immediately on seeing the *back* plates of the cuirasses, when masses of French infantry aproached with a heavy fire of musketry. They id " go through their work," as Napoleon often muttered, like no troops *he* had ever seen. Such were the deadly visits of the cannon and cavalry, that, as I have repeatedly been assured by officers with whom I have conver sed, these interludes of infantry battle were a kind of *refreshment*, after their toil with the other arms! They never took the trouble to look at their numbers; they felt as if boys had attacked them, just to keep them in wind; and invariably routed them by a very few steps of a run in advance with pointed bayonets. The Duke, in visiting different points, was almost invariably received with a shout of impatience to be led on. The gallant 95th were very tired of the iron cases, and the iron grape shot. An immense body of French infantry happened to approach that noble regiment at one time when Lord Wellington was paying them a visit, " Let us at 'em, my Lord," " let us down upon 'em," quite regardless of their numbers. " Not yet," replied the chief, " not yet, my brave men, but you shall have at them soon; firm a little longer; we *must not* be beat; what would they say in England?" The last caution was praise rather than encouragement; for,— let any people on earth match it, ancient or modern, from Thermopylè downwards, through

ages of Roman firmness and chivalrous enthusiasm,—in no part of the unconquerable line did a thought of flinching from his allotted spot, or of occupying any other ground *behind*, than the breadth of his back where he stood, if he should fall, find a moment's shelter in the mind of the poorest British soldier of Waterloo. The trite and abused term of glory does not convey the idea of a hundredth part of the merit of such unshaken constancy. " Les Anglais," says the intelligent author of the character of the different European armies, himself a Frenchman, " Les Anglais sont indu-
" bitablement le peuple le plus intrepide de
" l'Europe. Celui qui affronte la mort, et
" *la voit approcher*, avec le plus de sang froid
" d'indifference *."

From our vantage ground, we had gained a very satisfactory general idea of the field, and moved down to the farm house of La Haye Sainte, to examine the state in which

* The English are undoubtedly the most intrepid people in Europe. The people who meet as well as *wait for* death, with most of coolness and indifference.

the conflict had left that post, before we made a circuit for a more minute inspection of the field. Much of the wreck of the battle lay between the Duke of Wellington's station, and the farm house, which manifested the hazard to which he had been exposed. The " *Relation*" admits the necessity of sending against La Haye Sainte " nouvelle forces," before it was taken, by the slaughter of almost all its brave defenders. It is just an ordinary farm house, and court of offices. The house forms one side of a square, and the offices the other three; the court yard collecting the manure in the middle, and sheltering the cattle. The side opposite to the house is a long building for cows; the passage being separated from the cow's stalls by a parapet about four feet high. At each end of the passage is a large door or gate, both of which were literally riddled with musket balls, fired *from within* and *from without*, as could easily be distinguished from the kind of hole the ball had made. The bodies, after the action, were heaped up in the cow stalls, as high as the parapet. The whole farm house, yard, and offices might have afforded room for 1000 or 1500 men to act. They had made holes for musketry all around the place; and many a hole had been made for them by the enemy. The whole presented a scene of shattered ruin, which could not be looked upon without a degree of interest amounting to terror.

Some very poor children who seemed to starve about the ruins, soon joined us, and began to beg from us " quelque chose" with most persevering importunity. Their miserable appearance was in perfect agreement with the scene of desolation about them. We saw no grown people who seemed to have any interest in the premises. Having succeeded in opening the shattered door which led out to the fields to the west, we saw several women still engaged in the lately most lucrative occupation of gleaning up any thing which they could sell to strangers. The same persons had very probably been active in stripping and plundering the slain, before they were buried. We asked them where they were during the action:—" Toutes dans le bois*."—Did they

* " All in the wood."

hear the noise?—the answer was a shrug and look of dreadful recollection. They seemed to be finding very little worth lifting. We perhaps at that moment came in their way, for lying among some straw we found a French bayonet, evidently marked with blood, which we brought away with us.

We returned to the tree, and directed our steps westward to go along the British line to the right. There was no difficulty in tracing the line *by the graves* of the brave men who had fallen where they were first posted. The survivors never quitted it, but to advance. The very ground was hallowed; and it was trode by us with respect and gratitude; the multitudes below, so lately interred, occasioned a very impressive subject of reflection. If the unknown dead called forth these feelings, much more did the affecting consciousness of standing on the spot, where some one known to us had " nobly fought, and nobly died." We trode where the interesting Sir William De Lancy had met his death, when rallying, with great spirit and effect, a battalion of Hanoverians, who had got into confusion. He nobly refused to occupy the time of the surgeons with *his* wound, which he had heard them pronounce mortal, when they thought him insensible. He was removed to Brussels, where he died. This gallant young man's early name, and just favour with his great commander, excited general and deep interest for his fate; and no where more than in Edinburgh, where he had been married only a few weeks before.

Indeed the instances of heroic death were as numerous as they are affecting. Colonel Miller of the first guards requested a last sight of the colours under which he had fought. He kissed them fervently, and begged they might be waved over him till he expired.

The lamented Captain Curzon, Lord Scarsdale's son, met his fate with almost " military glee." In falling from his horse, he called out gaily to Lord March, who was riding with him at a gallop,—" Good bye, dear March." And by one effort more, when his friend had left him for the urgent duty of animating a foreign corps, in very critical circumstances, he looked up, and cried " Well done, dear March."

The nervous idea strongly occurred, of the next day's horrors of such a field as Waterloo. Numbers of the desperately wounded and dying, in the midst of the dead, raised their heads, when visitors to the scene passed them, to implore water, or to beg death at their hands, to end their agonies. Many of the wounded were not removed till the Wednesday, the third day after the battle.

All was now hushed in the stillness of a long line of graves, the sad consummation which the wounded implored. No one who has not seen it, can imagine how touching it is to see, strewed around their graves, fragments of what the brave men wore or carried when they fell. Among the straw of the trodden down corn, which still covered the field, lay caps, shoes, pieces of uniforms and shirts, tufts, cockades, feathers, ornamental horse-hair red and black, and what most struck us, great quantities of letters, and leaves of books. The latter were much too far defaced by rain and mud, to make it worth our while to lift any of them. In one letter, we could just make out the words, so affecting in the circumstances, " My dear husband." We brought away some leaves of a German hymn book; and probably, had we had time, might have found something curious in a department in which the peasants seemed not at all to have anticipated us.

We were now on the station of the Prince of Orange, and where he received his wound. The Dutch and Belgians under his immediate command behaved very gallantly. The Prince is said, in a moment of chivalrous feeling, when applauding their valour, to have torn the star from his breast, and thrown it into their column; adding, that he did not know who best deserved it, so he gave it among them.

A very gay regiment of gentlemen light horse volunteers, were in the battle of Waterloo, all inhabitants of a continental city, which I shall not name. An opportunity occurred for them to charge the French cavalry, and an aid-du-camp came to them with an order or request to that effect, from Lord Wellington. Their colonel in great surprise, objected the enemy's strength,—their cuirasses,—and the consideration, which had unaccountably, he said, escaped the Commander in Chief, that his regiment were all *gentlemen*. This diverting response, was carried back to Lord Wellington; who dispatched the messenger again to say, that if the *gentlemen* would take post upon an eminence, which he pointed to in the rear, they would have *an excellent view* of the battle; and he would leave the choice of a proper time to charge, entirely to their own sagacity and discretion, in which he had the fullest confidence! The colonel actually thanked the aid-du-camp, for this distinguished post of honour, and followed by his gallant train with their very high plumes, (the present great point of continental foppery), was out of danger in a moment.

A regiment of light dragoons of a very different stamp, the 12th, was posted near the Prince of Orange. Their charges were of the most spirited kind; and nothing but the cuirasses enabled the French dragoons to resist them. In the account of so much pure valour without trick or cover, against so much iron, it is not difficult to decide where honour would award the balance. Many brave men were sacrificed to the iron cases, and taffeta flags which frightened their horses. A gallant young friend of my own, lay near the spot we had now reached. He had just joined the 12th dragoons; and like a young soldier, was too forward in the first charge of his regiment, when he received his wound, which was instantly fatal. There was a melancholy satisfaction in beholding the spot of his honourable grave: A prouder sepulchre the turf on which the soldier falls, than the proudest mausoleum in consecrated ground.

No part of the field was more fertile in impressive associations, than the ground of the 30th, and I believe the 73d regiments, brigaded under our gallant countryman, severely wounded in the battle, Sir Colin Halket. I had already heard much of the firmness of these brave troops; and was to hear still more. To no square did the artillery, and particularly the cuirassiers, pay more frequent and tremendous visits; and never were they shaken for a moment.

Their almost *intimacy* with these death-bringing visitants, encreased so much as the day advanced, that they began to recognise their faces. Their boldness much provoked the soldiers. They galloped up to the bayonet points, where of course their horses made a full stop, to the great danger of pitching their riders into the square. They then rode round and round the fearless bulwark of bayonets; and in all the confidence of panoply, often coolly *walked* their horses, to have more time to search for some hole in the ranks, where they might ride in. The balls absolutely rung upon their mail; and nothing incommoded the rider, except bringing down his horse, which at last became the general order. In that event, he generally surrendered himself, and was received within the square, till he could be sent prisoner to the rear. A generosity ill-merited, when it is considered that the French spared very few lives, which it was in their power to take. Many officers were murdered, *after* giving up their arms; and when prisoners were collected, cavalry were sent to cut them down, when circumstances at the moment prevented their removal!

In the revolutionary demoralization, produced by an education of violence and selfishness, nothing is more frightful than the want of feeling which characterises the French soldiery. Their prisoners could hardly expect to be spared by the men, who lying wounded themselves, in the hospitals at Antwerp, were often seen mimicking the contortions of countenance, which were produced by the agonies of death, in one of their own comrades in the next bed. There is no curse to be compared to the *power* of fiends like these. Europe entire, was forced to put them down; and they made a gigantic effort at Waterloo to rise again. It makes one nervous to think that they were within a hair's-breadth of succeeding; and often I experienced a movement, in which it was hard to say, whether there was most of indignation or ridicule, when I heard Frenchmen and French-*women* lamenting in pathetic and *sentimental* terms, their failure; with scraps about " Vertu malheureuse, mais toujours respectable*."

The cuirassiers were repeatedly driven off by the 30th, and their sister regiment; reduced themselves by painful degrees, more and more every attack. Line was always again formed with unwearied alacrity; no complaint escaped the patient soldiers' lips, if we except an occasional cry to be led on. The storm was seen again gathering and rolling on. The serious command, " *re*-form square, prepare to receive cavalry," was promptly and accurately obeyed. The whole were prostrate on their breasts, to let the iron shower of artillery fly over, and erect in an instant, when the artillery ceased and the cavalry charged. Their country do not know one-tenth of the merit of " The men of Waterloo."

---

* Virtue unfortunate, but always respectable.

Unable to break in upon the square by open force, a commanding officer of cuirassiers tried a *ruse de guerre;* he lowered his sword to General Halket ; several of the officers called out " Sir, they surrender."— " Be firm and fire," was the promptly obeyed answer. The General justly suspected an offer of surrender to a body of infantry, fixed to the spot in a defensive position, by a body of cavalry, who had the option of galloping off, with all the plain open behind them. The volley sent the colonel and his cuirassiers, as usual, about, with a laugh of derision from the men he had meant to cut in pieces ; and many a ring from their balls, upon the back pieces of the mails.

This gallant brigade was honoured with several visits from the illustrious chief. In one he enquired " how they were." The answer was that two thirds of their number were down, and that the rest were so exhausted, that leave to retire, even for a short time, was most desirable ; some of the foreign corps, who had not suffered, to take their place. General H.

was told that the issue depended on the steady unflinching front of the British troops; and that even a change of place was hazardous in the extreme. He impressively said, "Enough, my lord, we stand here till the last man falls."

One anecdote more of this glorious brigade I cannot withhold. I have no apology to make for the length of my narrative; I feel that every one who reads of Waterloo, will agree with me in opinion, that it is impossible to dwell too long upon the engrossing theme. A gleam of the gentler affections is hailed with tenfold sympathy, when for a moment it gilds an interval of the empire of the sterner virtues in the warrior's bosom. It is like the breathing of the softest flute after the clang of a thousand trumpets; or the downy contact of the halcyon's breast which stills the stormy sea *. In the midst of their dangers, this band of heroes had their attention called to a very affecting scene of private friendship. Two of the officers were the more closely attached to

* Burke, in his bold figurative language, compared the kinder affections to " the soft green of the soul, on which the eye loves to repose."

each other, that they were not on terms of perfect good understanding with the rest of the mess; owing to their having opposed some arrangements which the rest thought expedient, but which it was expected would be attended with some expence. And at the same time concealed, most honourably, the real grounds of their opposition to the general voice; that besides their own families, they had each two sisters to support. A consideration which assuredly they could not have *pleaded* in vain. The similarity of their circumstances most naturally cemented their friendship; which was quite a bye-word in the regiment. After doing their duty calmly through nearly the whole of the murderous day, they found themselves both unhurt at a late hour in the evening; when one of them playfully called to the other, who stood at a little distance, " I always told you they never would hit me. They never did it in Spain; and they have not done it to-day." He had hardly spoke, when he was shot dead on the spot. His friend stood for a few moments motionless; then burst into tears; flew to the body, threw himself down beside it, and sobbed over it; inarticulately repeating several times, " My only friend." The officer who related the affecting story, told me, that so completely did the scene overcome every one who witnessed it, that there was not a dry eye among them.

There were not wanting some striking instances of individual heroism at Waterloo.

General Halket had a brother in the field, who was colonel of a Hanoverian corps, or a regiment of the German legion. A trait of spirit is related of him which has few examples in modern warfare; and is not exceeded by the far-famed atchievement of Robert Bruce in his short combat with Sir Henry Bohun, in that memorable battle, which stood foremost on history's brightest page, till Waterloo was fought. A French general was giving his orders with great confidence to a large body of French troops; and had come to their front unattended. Colonel Halket made a dash at him, having seized a favourable opportunity, at full gallop; and, putting a pistol to his breast, seized his horses reins, and brought him off from the very beards of his wonder-struck soldiers! I had the good fortune to spend an evening at the Hague with the mother and sister of these gallant men. From whom, it is needless to observe, I heard not one word of their deeds; which were quite new to me when I arrived at Brussels.

I had seen, as formerly mentioned, a young officer at Antwerp, who had received twenty-four sabre wounds. The 69th, his regiment, with another, was the square next on the right of general Halket's. In one of their formations the French cavalry was unfortunately too soon up for them, penetrated into the midst of them, and almost cut them to pieces.

We saw the point where a Belgic corps was stationed on the right, where the French called out, "Brave Belgians, come over and join your old comrades." It is well known they did not comply with the invitation.

We next in our interesting round, arrived at the memorable post of Hougomont, for ever associa ed with the name of the British foot guards. To them exclusively belongs the glory of having foiled the persevering and desperate attacks of at least 30,000 of the enemy; and they were just the *first*, *second*, and *third* regiment of guards. Here again national feelings were not to be resisted, Lord Saltoun, Colonels Home and M‘Donnell being of the " North Countrie," a nation (says the sweetest of their bards,)

> " Patient of toil; serene amidst alarms;
> " Inflexible in faith; invincible in arms."

We were surprised to find Hougomont, (or more correctly Gomont, a mistake of Lord Wellington's, destined now to perpetuity; and very naturally arising from hearing rapidly pronounced, *Le Chateau de Gomont*) a country seat with gardens neatly laid out in the Dutch taste, and extensive offices. A small wood was on the outside close to the high garden wall, which is of brick, perforated in two tiers for musketry; and shattered with the enemy's cannon balls. The light companies of the three regiments were in this wood, and were of course driven into the house.

The French officer's "*Relation*" admits that the place was not taken; that his countrymen suffered dreadfully in their unavailing attempts upon it, and at last endeavoured to shell it on fire. This they only partially effected; but they did leave the place a scorched and shattered inheritance, first to its brave defenders, and ultimately to its proprietor.

We could not resist picking up some small fragments even of the bricks and slates of this sacred spot; and we found some pieces of the bombs by which the chief havoc was occasioned. For some time after the battle, the accumulation of dead in and around this post presented perhaps the most shocking spectacle in the whole field. When in the garden, where fruit-trees and shrubberies seemed as if they were blighted, and the neat alleys of holly and yew have been much torn and deranged, we saw the poor gardener, who had remained in his garden all the time of the furious storm; because, as he candidly owned, after the battle was begun, he could not venture out of it; he confirmed the fact that the enemy never were within the premises; house, offices, or garden. It is said that two ladies, deeply interested for some relative, sat in a carriage the greatest part of the action, on the great road: certainly repeatedly under fire. And an old woman remained in her cottage almost in the midst of the fight, as she said, *to save* her cows and pigs! We did not see this heroine.

The natural idea of the indemnification of the owner of Hougomont occurred to us when we surveyed his roofless walls and desolate domain. One of the farmers of the field, the progress of which to harvest had been so tremendously interrupted, asked us whether the British government was to pay him for his corn which had been trodden down? We told him that the said government have sometimes paid much less reasonable costs; and that he should at least make the trial by putting in his claim.

The wood on the outside had been choaked up with the French dead; and more wreck lay here than on any part of the plain.

We crossed diagonally to the hovel of Belle Alliance, a name of superstitious coincidence; on which it is the custom of the French more than our's, to lay much stress. Certainly they never had three such names as *Fuentes d'Honoro*, *Vittoria*, and *Belle Alliance* to boast of! The house is of the poorest description; consisting of two rooms, with two smaller back rooms; a passage, and some miserable holes up stairs. There are also some ruinous outhouses, and a well into which several dead bodies were thrown. On the gable of the house, the owner has painted in very large and rude letters in black on a white-wash ground. " Hotel de la Belle Alliance!"

Our officer assured us, that Wellington and Blucher did *not* meet in this house, as generally believed; but some hundred yards further on in the pursuit. He had himself seen the meeting and the parting of these two great men, on that never to be forgotten occasion. It is possible the Duke may have entered the house; and the people shew a straw bottomed chair on which they say he sat down,—but at any rate it was the head quarters of Bonaparte during the battle. The latter had supped in one house, and slept in another, not far from Belle Alliance. The first of these houses had been unroofed and nearly destroyed, for no very assignable reason.

We entered the house, hovel as it was, with great respect; got some refreshment, and drank a bumper on the spot to *the alliance*. A party of Brussels inhabitants, whom we had often met on the field, were sharing the same bread and cheese, and *vin de pays*. There was no resisting a toast for them, " Vive le gallant Prince d'Orange, et les braves Belges qui se battoient à côte de lui, sur ce champ actuel*."

---

* Long live the gallant Prince of Orange, and the brave Belgians who fought by his side on this very field.

Their return was, "Vive le puissant Wellington et ses braves Anglais, nos meilleurs amis*."

We were so much in the spirit of the moment and place, as to read while we rested, both Lord Wellington and Bonaparte's account of the battle; which we had with us; and in the same paper there happened to be the account of the proceedings of the Edinburgh meeting for the Waterloo subscription. The speeches of several well known characters, and among the rest of Mr. Walter Scott, we read aloud; and certainly they could not have been read on a more impressive spot. —One extravagance further, and no more, we committed within the memorable walls of Belle Alliance. The passage was white-washed, and many names were written upon it; we quoted the following lines from the Vision of Don Roderick, on the very spot of Napoleon's final defeat and ruin, on his *first* trial of strength with " the Wellington." The

---

* Long live the powerful Wellington and his brave English, our best friends.

poet apostrophises Massena after the battle of Fuentes d'Honoro,

> " Tell him thy conqueror was Wellington;
> " And if he chafe be his *own* fortune tried,
> " God, and our cause, to aid, the venture we'll abide."

As we were so far advanced, we wished, before visiting Bonaparte's station and returning to the position of the left wing, to have one glance of the country over which the panic-struck enemy had fled. Nothing meets the eye but extensive uninclosed corn fields; with very little wood; as if Soigné had rendered all further plantation in its region unnecessary. There could not have been a clearer field for flight; and well the advantage was appreciated by every *individual* French soldier. It was in this quarter the Prussian stragglers were most dangerous for several days after the battle.

The officer who was with us belonged to the 23d regiment. His regiment passed close to Belle Alliance on the opposite side of the road; by which means he was witness to what Lord Wellington even *said* to Blucher. He saw them meet on the road, and walk their horses for some hundred yards in earnest conversation; when Lord Wellington wished the veteran good night and success in the pursuit; and turned his horse back again to Waterloo to write his important despatches.

For a great breadth along the road, our officer pointed out to us the station of the reserve of the cavalry of the old guard; with which a desperate final effort was made to retrieve the battle. The marks of the horses feet in the deep ground, hardened again when we saw it, gave an amazing idea of the immensity of the force which had stood there. The reserve of the young guard was posted in a hollow between Belle Alliance and Mon Plaisir. To the right o the 23d, advanced in the pursuit the 52d and 71st regiments. It fell to them to meet the young guard. Numbers were more than ever out of the question—panic had spread through the vast hordes of the enemy. The two regiments, weakened as they had been, rushed upon the guards, and routed them in an instant; the same guard with whose spirit and equipment, Napoleon had so lately before made all Europe to resound. A most admirable manœuvre was here performed by the two victorious regiments. They separated, and running on two sides of an oval, for a considerable way, met again; and thus cut off several thousand prisoners.

Returning by Belle Alliance, we advanced about 150 yards to the rising ground, on the left hand side of the road, looking to the British army, from which Napoleon viewed the field; and a very complete view he had of it. He had no scaffold erected where he stood, and certainly never went after the battle had commenced, to the telegraph in the rear, which was at the distance of at least a mile. The " *Relation*" says, that he was generally dismounted, walking backwards and forwards in his usual attitude, with his hands behind his back, and looking stedfastly at the conflict. Lacoste the farmer, or rather proprietor of Belle Alliance, it is well known, was pinion-

VISIT TO THE FIELD. 103

ed, set on horseback, and placed beside the Emperor; very often exposed to fire, and laughed at for manifesting very natural alarm, carried off for some miles in the flight, when the Emperor used the freedom to forget him; and ultimately dismissed with the high reward for all he had undergone, of one Napoleon d'or, about 20s. Sterling. We had the good fortune to see this man. By the concurring testimony of friends as well as enemies, the great Napoleon forfeited his name on the spot of ground where we now stood. With all his pretensions to consummate skill, he had but one *tactique*, and that was furious onset with overpowering masses of force; a system which had in no previous battle, Leipsic excepted, ever failed him. He was well aware of the numerical inferiority of the British army, and making every allowance for their determined valour, well known, but yet untried by him, he concluded confidently, that as they must remain on the defensive, a sufficient quantity of grape shot, would, in a certain number of hours, entirely cut them down.

His ignorant surprise has already been mentioned, and pretended joy to see the English faced about at all; his exclamation " Ah ! I have them yet," evidently shewed that he had never fought them before. Lacoste describes his agitation as extreme, and his consumption of snuff inordinate, when the three mighty armies which he had rolled on to Hougomont, La Haye Sainte, and the British left, failed to produce the result of French onset, to which *he* had been accustomed.—Two were defied and visited with frightful carnage ; and one was recoiling in confusion; and they comprised more than half his vast army. He became cross and short in his answers; and furious in his commands. He had however no want of troops. For six hours more, with his usual profligate disregard of human life, he varied not the mode of attack, but poured his devoted enthusiasts on, though again and again driven back with immense slaughter. La Haye Sainte was taken, half a mile in his front along the road. It was of no use but to enclose the captors for the well directed range of the British howitzers. A message came from the general, for orders about that useless post; which could not be kept because of *a battery* which commanded it; what would it please his Majesty to order the general to do? " S'en emparer*," was the laconic answer, and the Emperor turned his back on the aide-du-camp.

He could not restrain occasional compliments to the British troops.—" How they form,—how they move,—how they do their work,—what beautiful troops."

About this time, nearly four o'clock in the afternoon, a British officer was brought into his presence a prisoner. He was severely wounded, but as it is an important rule in battle to transmit prisoners of rank to head quarters, he was detained till several questions were put to him by the Emperor, and, as I was informed, with great politeness.

1*st*. " Is Lord Wellington himself in the field?"—*Ans*. " He is."

" Carry it."

2*d.* " What is the state of the spirits of the English troops ?"—*Ans.* " As determined as ever."

3*d.* " Where are the Prussians ?"—*Ans.* " It is believed they are at hand."

Bonaparte was observed to look thoughtful. He however politely dismissed the officer, to have his wounds taken care of.

The British keeping their defensive position, the entire French army, as the assailants, naturally found themselves very considerably advanced on the plain; an advance which Bonaparte falsely called occupying the British *line.* This very advance was their ruin. The British artillery now played from their higher ground upon the whole French army, with the exception of the reserve of guards old and young; and every opportunity of attack was seized by both British infantry and cavalry. " The combat deepened," and fresh spirits rushed " to glory or the grave." It was now the tug of battle:—The impetuosity, the high spirit, the " stern joy," of first onset was gone by; now was come the murderous strain of the mighty armies, the poise and balance of the day.

" The affair is kept up," (*se soutient*) says the " *Relation*,"—" not a foot on either side " is yielded; new columns advance; charges " are renewed; three times the position is on " the point of being forced; and three times, " after prodigies of valour, the French are " stopped short."

Nothing can be more descriptive than what follows of the re-action, the languor, which succeed over-excitement; the depression of baulked enthusiasm.

" Hesitation appeared in the French army, " and marked uneasiness *(vives inquietudes.)* " Some dismounted batteries retired, multi- " tudes of wounded separate from the co- " lumns, and spread alarm for the issue of " battle. Profound silence had succeeded to " the acclamations and cries of joy of the sol- " diers, sure of being led to victory. At the " moment *all* the troops, with the exception of " the infantry of the guard, were engaged and

" exposed to a fire the most murderous. The
" action continued with the same violence, but
" led to no result.

" *It was near seven o'clock.* Bonaparte, who
" till that moment had remained on the ridge
" which he had chosen, and from which he saw
" well all that passed, contemplated with a
" look of ferocity, the hideous prospect of so
" frightful a butchery. The more the obsta-
" cles multiplied, the more he became obsti-
" nate. He was indignant at the unforeseen
" difficulties; and, far from having fears to
" devote an army, whose confidence in him
" had no bounds, he persevered in sending on
" fresh troops, with orders to march forward,
" to charge with the bayonet, to sweep away.
" Several times he was told from different
" points, that the affair was against him, that
" the troops appeared to be shaken; ' en
" avant,' repondit-il, ' en avant,'—*forward,
" forward.*"

Another British officer was brought prisoner at this rare juncture; and witnessed the
unexpected demeanour of this hitherto ido-

lized man, in the presence of an enemy so new to him. He raved and stormed, and, regardless of witnesses, threw away in a moment the character founded on fifteen years of miracles. A British officer witnessed this suicide of Napoleon's fame; and saw his star set for ever, before the glorious ascendant of his own country. It was, it may be believed, delightful to this officer, to hear the answer given to Bonaparte's general wholesale commands, to *destroy* and *break* and *sweep away* the English. " Sire, il est impossible." Yet at the very moment he was sending off estaffettes with despatches; and, true to the last gasp of his political existence, to that lying policy which has itself roused the vengeance of united Europe, he repeated several times, " avec destraction, Qu'il n'oublie pas de dire partant que la victoire est à moi*." Several officers near him expressed their wonder, by saying, " Il a perdu la tête†."

* " With distraction, Let him not forget to say every where, that the victory is mine."
† " The man is mad."

How different this melancholy scene of the fury of disappointed oppression, from the *calm* he pretended at Jena! when he played the unruffled god, far above the passions of the war below, and its vulgar risks; on a safe eminence, waving his baton, and columns of the enemy disappeared! It is indeed time that this mummery, this serenity of triumphant profligacy should be exposed in all its hollow worthlessness and naked deformity.

The Prussians appeared. From the ground on which we stood, the wood seemed about three miles off, from which they began to debouche about seven o'clock in the evening. Lacoste witnessed the information repeatedly brought to Bonaparte, and heard his persevering assertion, that it was the corps of Marshal Grouchy. This, however, was not his real belief; for, instead of waiting for it, he immediately resolved to throw his last stake, before the *possible* Prussians might arrive. The old and middle guard were now ordered forward, as the last column of attack. It was led by Ney, as he himself narrates, in mournful silence, to make a *last* desperate effort on the British center and left: he well knowing all the time that the battle was already lost, and could not be retrieved by a mere reserve, if the whole army had failed to make any impression on the British position. The lamented Sir Thomas Picton was to meet and confound this last effort of rage and despair, but not to survive his triumph.

We left the station of Bonaparte, and in imagination, as we proceeded, attended the sullen march of this column to the point of its destined defeat. The whole French army had been premonished of the movement of the old guard; and new and desperate efforts were put in requisition: all eyes were fixed on the old guard, which had never before failed. New efforts *were* made, in a surprising degree, all along the line, by this inflammable volatile soldiery. The flame of honour burned, however, much more steadily in the British line. Great efforts in their enemies, as usual produced still greater in them, and not an inch was gained by the assailants. The ground over which the guard moved, and over which they fled, was still, when we passed it, covered by their spoil, and marked by horses' feet, cannon wheels, and the deeper furrows of balls and bombs. On no part of the field did we see more extended marks of blood. As usual, the artillery of the guard poured its iron shower, and the cavalry followed with their desperate charge. It is in vain for Bonaparte to say, that his old guard were not beaten, or that the cry to which he attributes his defeat, " the old guard are driven back," was not true. The bold movement of Picton, with his favourite Highlanders, was once more tried, and, after the British artillery had done their part, the boasted cavalry of the old imperial guard were charged and routed by the Scottish bayonet! We stood with exquisite national feelings here. From this point, as Lord Wellington's despatch states, commenced that final and fatal recoil, which determined him to give the order for a general attack by the whole army. The infantry rushed down the slope, in pur-

VISIT TO THE FIELD. 113

suit of their advantage. An immense mass of the grenadiers of the guard stood yet unbroken in their front. The Greys once more appeared; and, impatient to support their countrymen, leapt their horses, almost one by one, through the gaps in the hedge, hardly waited to form, but galloped down into the middle of the Highlanders, cheering " *Scotland for ever!*" the watch word spread, and electrified the whole with a phrenzy of ardour, and the old guard fled in irretrievable rout before them. Ney, by his own account, dismounted, fled on foot, from what *he* calls this *terrible* battle, and, unhappily for himself, escaped;— while Picton,

" With his back to the ground, and his feet to the foe,
" Leaving in battle no blot on his name,
" Look'd proudly to heaven, from the death-bed of fame."

A thousand French *dead*, alone, lay on this spot; and even yet it exhibited holsters, (one we picked up filled with dried blood,) standard holders, pieces of bridles, straps, girths, &c. all denoting a tremendous conflict of cavalry;

and the ground seemed quite cut to pieces with marks of the *struggling* exertions of horses' feet. The well-known caps of the grenadiers of the French guard, lay yet in considerable numbers; with rags of their uniforms, and some more affecting remains were also there, pieces of tartan and of black ostrich feathers, once worn by our gallant countrymen *.

A loud cheer, we were informed by our officer, now ran along the whole British line. He was much struck by observing the sun shine out at the moment, after having been some

---

* In addition to Marshal Blucher's testimony in his despatch, that the old guard "were baffled by the intrepidity of the Scottish regiments," it was most flattering to hear the truth of this almost miraculous conduct of our countrymen, confirmed by the prevailing belief both in Paris and on the road to it, in consequence of what was told by the French soldiers themselves, that it was the Scotch troops who chiefly occasioned the loss of the battle, by defeating the old guard. The impression they have made in Paris itself, fully justifies their belief on the subject. Tartan is a prevailing fashion with the ladies; and the full garb is employed as an attraction by wax-work exhibitors. I saw it repeatedly introduced on the stage with great applause.

VISIT TO THE FIELD. 115

hours under cloud! In an instant the whole was on the forward move. The British guards had destroyed a column of the old guard, in their own front, near Hougomont. The enemy were already in irretrievable rout. The feeble attempt, made in phrenzy, by Bonaparte with the young guard, is not worth mentioning: the "*Relation*" says, they turned with the torrent. The indescribable anxieties of the British chief were now over. They had been almost too much to be born. Often he had prayed in agony, for the Prussians or the night! When their guns commenced, it is described by officers who heard it, as something like a *yell* of rapture, with which he called out, "There goes old Blucher at last," and unable to bear up longer, burst into tears. 15,000 of his friends lay on the ground about him; and before him was the spectacle of his powerful enemy, who were within a hairsbreadth of destroying him, in full rout and ruin;—and the world delivered!—The moment was too overpowering, the feeling too big for any heart to contain. In an instant the great Napoleon and France, were levelled in the dust. Marengo, Austerlitz, Jena, Friedland, Wagram, fell " like stars from the firmament cast,"—" the star of Peace" arose—Its enemies were a mass of panic and impotency—The "meteor flag of England" was burning terrific, and had consigned to insulted injured Prussia, a ripened harvest of revenge.

The mind has scarcely buoyancy sufficient to allot to England a pinnacle of glory high enough for the crisis at this moment produced. The account is too complex, as well as too vast, to give at one view a grasp of all its details and elements.

One feature is in prominent and brilliant light, the *Steadiness* of England for five and twenty years; concentrated into a focus of virtue at Waterloo, to which eternal justice denied not the victory. How she has snatched from the humbled head of France, that usurped crown which so ill became her—the badge which belongs to the *true* " *grand nation*,"— and with united consent of Europe, put it on her own!

VISIT TO THE FIELD. 117

What would Cowper now have said, when he did such justice to the unconquerable steadiness of his country when bearing up against the jealousy and hostility of the world; instead of engrossing, as she now does, their gratitude and admiration.

"O England, thou art a devoted deer,
"Beset by every ill but that of fear.
"The nations hunt, all mark thee for a prey,
"They swarm around thee, but thou standst at bay;
"Undaunted still, tho' wearied and perplexed,
"Once Chatham saved thee, Who shall save thee next!"

A noble proof occurred in the evening of the battle, of the generous candour of the brave Prussians themselves, on the question of British ascendancy. A regiment of light dragoons, overtook a corps of Prussian cavalry in the pursuit. The latter instantly formed line to give the British the lead; and, as they passed to take the compliment, the Prussian trumpets sounded God save the King, with loud huzzas! There are some junctures in human affairs, which are almost too much for the feelings.

We saw the extreme left; the well defended post of the brave men, who had " whetted their swords on Brunswick's tomb." Their conduct in the battle was not surpassed even by that of the British. They had lost their gallant Prince two days before, and mourning, which their uniform is, still worn for the aged Duke, who died of his wounds and a broken heart after the day of Jena, well became the double vengeance which was claimed from them at Waterloo; and honourably they paid the debt.

There is no better witness to the entire rout of the French army than the author of " *The Relation.*"—" The army now quit spon-
" taneously and at the same instant its ground,
" and scatter like a torrent; the cannoneers
" abandon their guns, the soldiers of the train
" cut the traces of their horses, the infantry,
" the cavalry, all the arms are mingled and
" confounded, presenting now only an un-
" formed mass, which nothing could arrest,
" and which was intent on saving itself by the
" road and across the fields. A vast number

" of carriages in park along the sides of the
" road, followed the movement with precipita-
" tion, crowded to the road, and encumbered
" it to such a degree, that not a wheel could
" move.

" No point of direction had been given,
" and no word of command could now be
" heard. The generals, and other chiefs, lost
" in the crowd, and carried along with it,
" were separated from their troops. There
" was no longer a single battalion to rally up-
" on ; and since nothing had been provided
" to insure a reasonable retreat, how was it
" possible to resist a derout so complete, of
" which no idea could have been formed,
" and which was *till then* unheard of in the
" French army, already visited by so many
" disasters.

" The guard, that immoveable phalanx,
" which in the greatest catastrophes had been
" the rallying point of the army, and its ram-
" part ; the guard, in fine, the terror of the
" enemy, was overthrown *(terrassée,)* and fled

"dispersed with the multitude! Every one "saved himself as he best could, *(au hazard)* "&c."

The Frenchman's account of the spirit of the pursuit is equally picturesque.

But where was Napoleon? Reports were various in the flying army about him. That he had fallen—that he was taken. He was neither the one nor the other. Lacoste first gives evidence on the subject, and it is impossible to imagine more damning testimony against the Emperor. His remark repeatedly was, " we must save *ourselves.*"—" How terrible these grey horses are.—We must save *ourselves.*" The man that had squandered the lives of millions, and wrung tears from every eye on the Continent of Europe, " Who never had pity on any one," " nor looked on what he trode !" Yet Frederick of Prussia retrieved a battle in circumstances fully as desperate. Instead of " we must save ourselves;" he galloped to a small but firm body of his guards, the only remnant of the field, and calmly asked them, " My friends, when do you mean to die?"—" Now!" was the answer.—" Then follow me*!"

Napoleon availed himself of the darkness and the crowd, and sneaked away. It was extreme bad taste in the recent conqueror of the world. It would have been quite suitable in a pick-pocket; but it woefully misbecame an Emperor. The Greys should have been Napoleon's last resource; a death like Argentine's, if not a cast like Frederick's. He was soon recognised in the crowd, according to " *The Relation*," and sadly disquieted to hear " l'Empereur." He was known by his gray capote, or great-coat, and his dappled horse, (*cheval pommelè*.) This did not suit his *project* of saving himself, and he went from one crowd to another, repeatedly recognised, to his great inconvenience. The question of his poor disposition to cling to life, however degraded, is certainly now at rest. The man who, when the lives of

---

* I was told this singular anecdote by a Prussian officer in Paris.

others were concerned, could only cry, "*en avant, en avant,*" when his *own* came to be the question, " we must save ourselves!" Napoleon himself then, is the only person in his army *convicted* of having cried " sauve qui peut," a charge he brings against the army which he sacrificed; but which is indignantly repelled by Marshal Ney, in his justification. The degraded emperor was received into Phillipville, after having been subjected to the most mortifying verification at the gate. The report having spread that he was in the town, a number of his *even yet* attached soldiers, collected on the outside of the walls, to shed their blood for him. This was most inexpedient, for it involved the possible shedding of his own. It was urgent to get quit of these troublesome devotees, whose *attroupement* would assuredly bring the enemy. The great Napolean *managed* that, by ordering a cry to be raised, of which he had seen the effect in Russia, " Voila les Cossacs! vite, vite, voila les Cossacs!" This interesting manœuvre was completely successful. The emperor got safe out of the town; but was most unlucky in being again recognised as he passed Rocroi, with that to him *most offensive* cry of "vive l'Empereur;" notwithstanding of which, he arrived safe and sound, (plein de vie et de santé), among the inhabitants of his good city of Paris. " O honte eternelle! (says the author of *The Relation*), comment peindre l'indignation dont ils durent être pénétres* !"

It is high time that mankind should have done with conquerors, and conquerors like Bonaparte.

He is reported to have said in his affected oracular manner, on landing from Elba at Frejus, "Voila le congres dissous." And now that we have seen the annihilation of the last remnant of the hordes, who have so long sustained him and his system; the reins drop for ever from his hands, palsied by the judgment of Heaven; we may say with Megret,

---

* " O eternal disgrace! how is it possible to depict the indignation they must have felt."

when he heard of the death of Charles XII. by a cannon ball at Frederickstadt,

"Voila la piece finie."—*Behold the play at an end.*

I found myself on the field, nearly half an hour after the rest of our party, with imagination even yet unsatisfied, and associations as active as ever. I was now alone on the silent scene; with a distant view of some poor peasant still patiently plying the trade of relic hunting. It was the grave of 20,000 men, who, little more than a month before, had descended into the magnificent arena, full of life and hope. It is impossible to describe the sort of feeling resulting from the idea of the vast charnel house around.

All about lay the melancholy remains of the clothes, accoutrements, books, and letters of the dead. The two last after the interment, were spread over the field, like the rubbish of a stationer's shop.

One moment more on the probable spot where Lord Wellington was encircled by a square for a considerable time, with the French

---

* A gentleman in Brussels shewed me an interesting relic of this sort of spoil, found on the spot now described; a coarsely printed copy of Scotch songs, and some leaves of a pocket bible.

cuirassiers on the outside; and I left the field, prouder of the name of Briton, than on any moment of self-gratulation on the same score, during my life.

On joining my friends, I found one of them had bought a cuirass and brace of beautiful pistols, of very considerable value, which the poor woman who sold them had found in the cloak-case of a French general. She paid a compliment to England, the sincerity of which she proved by the act with which it was accompanied. We happened to have no other coin but guineas to pay the purchase. The price was three. When she saw the coins she refused them; not because she thought them bad money, but because she had never seen them before. We assured her that in Brussels she could, at the time, exchange them for twenty-six francs each.—She still hesitated, and urged her poverty if we should deceive her. All at once however she took the money, adding, " Eh bien! Vous êtes Anglais, et les Anglais ne trompent jamais*."

* " Very well! You are English, and the English never deceive."

It was just the nation of which such a character prevailed so universally as to have reached a poor Belgic peasant, for which was reserved, in the justification of the ways of heaven to man, the victory of Waterloo.

CONCLUSION.

When detailing examples of the firmness of the British troops through the whole of the day of Waterloo, I purposely postponed some reflections which at the time forcibly presented themselves; that neither description nor narrative might suffer by interruption.

The author of "the Character of the European armies" gives to the British the credit, as formerly stated, of being the most intrepid people in Europe. It is a higher feeling than national vanity which prompts me to apply this opinion by asserting, that no nation in Europe would have triumphed, in the circumstances, at Waterloo but the British—Certainly the French least of any: They have not the steady principle. Well their leaders know, that to wait attack with them is always unsafe, and generally fatal. To the momentum of their enthusiasm motion is necessary —the excitement, the *abandon*, of forward overwhelming attack. The artificial stimulus of shouts and acclamations, *carries* the French troops, and there follows a descent to a very ordinary character when the excitement fails or the impetus is jarred or curtailed of its full swing, by resistance. It is a finally hopeless expedient in such a crisis, to draw the engine back, to be wound up and let off again and again with decreasing force.

The English character, on the other hand, is intrinsically strong;—it is self-contained—it needs no external impulse—It therefore *defends* as effectually as it assails. This difference was strongly marked throughout the peninsular war, but never more strongly than at Waterloo. When the French were *attacked* they were broken, and they fled from very

CONCLUSION.

inferior numbers, which had stood their utmost efforts for ten hours.

It is impossible to imagine a more impressive picture than such a soldiery presents, of the exalted *morale* of a high-minded cultivated people. A manly energy invigorates every part of their system, civil and military. It is a magnificent effect of the progressive improvement of centuries, without one retrograde step. In their undertakings, individual or national, failure *must not* be. There is a rivalry in the race of improvement, which ensures success. The soldier of such a country must be invincible. His energy is just a portion directed to his own vocation of the steady enterprise which is found in every other. If his enemy makes great efforts, he must just make greater,

" His spirit rising as his toils increase."

" *He must not be beaten.*" He is at the same time perfectly assured that, in the battle, the same determination actuates his right and left-hand neighbours; he can rely upon them as long as they keep their recollection and their feet. In aid of all, comes the conclusion of his cooler moments, that firmness is his only safety—that flight is almost certain destruction—that it is much wiser to drive off the danger than to turn a defenceless back upon it. Yet does this compound of feeling and reasoning belong to a people of a very superior order alone. It is principle and good sense; totally different from the habit, the superstition, or the attachment, which rivets the Russian to the spot allotted him in a state of comparative insensibility or passive endurance; and brave and spirited as are the Prussian and Austrian, it is but lately that they have been brought to the practical conclusion that it is really possible to make head against Frenchmen: A spell, thank heaven, broken now for ever.—But at no time of the long war did the British soldier, more than the British sailor, hesitate an instant; and although the mighty *system* of France often obliged him to retreat before her overwhelm-

CONCLUSION.

ing power, he never *actually fought* in vain. It is a salutary truth, for the benefit of ages yet to come, that the French least of any people possess this respectable steadiness.—Defending fortifications is not here in question; but in the fair onset of the open field, they have *always* fled from a spirited and determined attack; when their enemies were at all in numbers approaching to their own. From Maida to Waterloo, there has not been one example of their repelling it. They have made no figure since the snows of Russia brought their armies down to the numbers of their enemies. The overpowering force of their previous campaigns always gave them the choice of being the assailants. In Spain they were confounded with *the attacks* at Salamanca and Vittoria. If there were no other solution, the contrasted character of the British and French armies, or which is the same thing, of the British and French people, would at once determine on which side is the great, the good, the just cause.—Which rushed with profligate ferocity to destroy—which stood with unshaken constancy to preserve the peace of the world. One hour of the virtue of Waterloo eclipses twenty noisy years of French triumph; turns their *glory* into a term of ridicule; and veils all the pillars and arches of victory that ever deluded themselves or insulted the world.

Without refusing to the brave Prussians any part of the high credit due to the service which their exertions at Waterloo have rendered to mankind, we may, without vain glory, rejoice that the power of Britain, *single-handed*, has been so satisfactorily displayed.

It is of vital consequence to the European cause that the fact should be universally admited, that England, with hardly one fifth part of her regular force, was strong enough *alone* to defeat the finest army of France*. The reviving presumption of the French would have been in the precise proportion of the extent of the force which was necessary to put

* It is usual for the Parisians to tell the Prussians, when they *dare* use the freedom, that they only picked up the game which the English killed.

them down; and no view of the matter can be conceived more unfavourable, than that the grand victory had been *de facto* gained by the *whole million* of the enemies of France, which have at last poured into her bosom; and she thereby left in the belief that she would not have been humbled, and therefore never will again, without the assemblage of the whole world against her, in its present admirable equipment and unqualified co-operation.

It is just the finest feature of the Wellingtonian victory, that the future security of the world is now advanced incalculably, from where it was left last year by the combinations of Leipsic. If a single power baffled the utmost efforts of France, that power itself will in future go far to keep her in check, and prevent the destruction of any other, before a coalition can be formed. To none of the powers was it of more real consequence that this chance should fall, than to Great Britain; the nearest and most active neighbour of France. The blood which it has cost,— blood which has not sunk into the barren sand—might have been poured out less profusely, had the Prussian army come up in the morning, rather than in the evening; but the moral effect on men's estimates of the result, and especially on the French themselves, would have been immeasurably less favourable to the future equilibrium, and consequent peace of Europe.

It is very commonly said and believed, that had Bonaparte directed his whole force against the Duke of Wellington first, he would have destroyed him; and the omission of this is charged against him by Marshal Ney, as his grand error. No doubt, 150,000 men would have born very hard on 80,000, with their newly raised auxiliaries, attacked too before they were concentrated. But this is altogether an unfair manner of comparing the soldiers of Great Britain and France. If we take the battle of Waterloo as it was, there occurs a much fairer.——

Suppose first, That the 80,000 men under Lord Wellington's command, had been *all British*; the French still 130,000.——

Suppose second, That our army had been 130,000 : equal numerically to the French ; and *all British*——

Suppose third, That the French had just exchanged relative situations with the British, and with 30,000 French and 50,000 foreigners, it had been *their* task to make head against 130,000 *all British!*—It is asked what would have been the progressive saving of time to the British army, on the 18th of June, in these three cases respectively?

Except when driven to it, as I sometimes found myself during my visit to Paris, the above were not suppositions, which, in civility, I could offer for the rumination of Frenchmen with whom I conversed. I kept them, however, as a never-failing reserve to abridge discussions of this kind, when, without being sought by me, they came in my way. But they must not be forgotten, either on the Continent or at home, in estimating the victory of Waterloo; for they are just the considerations which confer upon that victory its full effect on the future security of the world; and *à for-*

tiori when it is considered, that by directing her well-awakened attention to that branch of her power, there is nothing to prevent England, if unfortunately she shall be called upon to go to war again, to produce an army on the Continent, of at least 100,000 men all British; a force, we are well entitled to conclude, strong enough for any purpose whatever.

Moral reflections on the Grand Interposition of Waterloo, are for ever conflicting in the mind, and injuring its power of discriminate and satisfactory consideration. The thought by far the most prominent, is the speed of the course which has been run—" the fell swoop" which in an instant, like the judgments of heaven when punishing by miracle, has made *such* an enemy to vanish, and wrought *such* a change in the face of human affairs. What has been effected? A few short days before, Europe entire was dazzled with the spectacle of the throne of Napoleon Bonaparte

CONCLUSION. 137

again erected, as if by enchantment, more towering than ever. The ascent crowded with the princes of his dynasty, and captains of his host; itself in countless numbers, encircling its chief, enthusiastic in his cause to desperation and phrenzy, and conducting the electrical ardour to sympathising, applauding, undoubting millions around. Armies on armies rolling on to the scene; and oaths and shouts from a people of power which had often shaken Europe to its extremes, astounding the world, and making the stoutest hearts to fear for the issue of the conflict about to be renewed.

A few moments before, and language could hardly furnish them terms of sufficient confidence, defiance, and vengeance.—" We shall not soon hear again of the Prussians, and as for the English we shall now see what will become of them. The Emperor is here *."

Where is the Emperor now? Where is his mighty army? Where is the beautiful,

---

* French letters from the field, immediately before the battle.

the invincible, the sacred France? Never was there so short a space between the highest presumption and the lowest prostration; between an attitude which was the terror, and a humiliation which is the bye-word of nations. It is no vain glory when Britain, who dealt the blow, exults; as would have been the shout of France had the victory been hers. It is no triumph over an unfortunate and virtuous people. She triumphs because sound principle is vindicated, and the times restored when Justice has again some chance of making her voice heard in the world.

Last of all, has one blow from England, launched from his pinnacle the almost deified captain of the long invincible soldiery of France ; and forced him, with an inapplicable scrap of sentiment about Themistocles in his mouth, to bow his head to her grandeur, and mendicate his life from her mercy! No part of the *denouement* of the wondrous drama has more astonished the French people and exalted England in their eyes, than that charm of hers, that spell of her power, which

CONCLUSION. 139

has drawn the god of their senses and imaginations, their Emperor, by, to them, something like supernatural fascination and fatality, absolutely into her own hands, to fix his destiny for ever.

Had all been reversed,—had France overwhelmed England, language is in vain searched for a term to qualify the injury such a melancholy event would have effected to the great cause of humanity. The thought cannot be endured for a moment!—the victory of France over England!—the triumph once more, and the long reign for generations, of profligacy and cruelty, gilded over by fine sentiment: with the words without the meaning of most exalted virtue: while honour and principle were driven to a doubtful, at least permanent struggle, for their own existence, losing rank and estimation every hour among mankind. No interposition of the God of battles could have bestowed such a gift on humanity as the reunion of power with right; the heart-reviving combination of real military and national glory with the less ostentatious but more substantial virtues which morals and religion recommend; and which have shewn that they can neither be talked, nor laughed, nor fought out of fashion —a combination from which France herself, as most she needs,—will yet most benefit; when the ruffian violence, the knavery, and the pretensions of her revolution are remembered only as a dreadful warning to mankind.

APPENDIX.

LONDON GAZETTE EXTRAORDINARY.

Downing Street, June 22, 1815.

Major the Honourable H. Percy, arrived late last night with a dispatch from Field Marshal the Duke of Wellington, K. G. to Earl Bathurst, his Majesty's Principal Secretary of State for the War Department, of which the following is a copy:

Waterloo, June 19, 1815.

MY LORD,

Bonaparte having collected the 1st, 2d, 3d, 4th, and 6th corps of the French army and the Imperial Guards, and nearly all the cavalry, on the Sambre, and between that river and the Meuse, between the 10th and the 14th of the month, advanced on the 15th and attacked the Prussian posts at Thuin and Lobez, on the Sambre, at daylight in the morning.

I did not hear of these events till the evening of the 15th, and I immediately ordered the troops to prepare to march; and afterwards to march to the left, as soon as I had intelligence from other quarters to prove that the enemy's movement upon Charleroi was the real attack.

The enemy drove the Prussian posts from the Sambre on that day; and General Ziethen, who commanded the corps which had been at Charleroi, retired upon Fleurus; and Marshal Prince Blucher concentrated the Prussian army upon Sombreffe, holding the villages in front of his position of St. Amand and Ligny.

The enemy continued his march along the road from Charleroi towards Brussels, and on the same evening, the 15th, attacked a brigade of the army of the Netherlands, under Prince de Weimar, posted at Frasne, and forced it back to the farm-house on the same road, called Les Quatre Bras.

The Prince of Orange immediately reinforced this brigade with another of the same division, under General Perponcher; and, in the morning early, regained part of the ground which had been lost, so as to have the command of the communication leading from Nivelles and Brussels, with Marshal Blucher's position.

In the meantime I had directed the whole army to march upon Les Quatre Bras, and the 5th divi-

BATTLE OF WATERLOO. 143

sion, under Lieutenant General Sir Thomas Picton, arrived at about half-past two in the day, followed by the corps of troops under the Duke of Brunswick, and afterwards by the contingent of Nassau.

At this time the enemy commenced an attack upon Prince Blucher with his whole force, excepting the 1st and 2d corps; and a corps of cavalry under General Kellerman, with which he attacked our post at Les Quatre Bras.

The Prussian army maintained their position with their usual gallantry and perseverance, against a great disparity of numbers, as the 4th corps of their army, under General Bulow, had not joined, and I was not able to assist them as I wished, as I was attacked myself, and the troops, the cavalry in particular, which had a long distance to march, had not arrived.

We maintained our position also, and completely defeated and repulsed all the enemy's attempts to get possession of it. The enemy repeatedly attacked us with a large body of infantry and cavalry, supported by a numerous and powerful artillery; he made several charges with the cavalry upon our infantry, but all were repulsed in the steadiest manner. In this affair, his Royal Highness the Prince of Orange, the Duke of Brunswick, and Lieutenant General Sir Thomas Picton, and Major-General Sir James Kempt, and Sir Denis Pack, who were engaged from the commencement of the enemy's attack, highly distinguished themselves, as well as Lieutenant General Charles Baron Alten, Major General Sir C. Halket, Lieutenant-General Cooke, and Major-Generals Maitland and Byng, as they successively arrived. The troops of the 5th division, and those of the Brunswick corps, were long and severely engaged, and conducted themselves with the utmost gallantry. I must particularly mention the 28th, 42d, 78th, and 92d regiments, and the battalion of Hanoverians.

Our loss was great, as your lordship will perceive by the inclosed return; and I have particularly to regret His Serene Highness the Duke of Brunswick, who fell, fighting gallantly, at the head of his troops.

Although Marshal Blucher had maintained his position at Sombref, he still found himself much weakened by the severity of the contest in which he had been engaged, and, as the fourth corps had not arrived, he determined to fall back, and concentrated his army upon Wavre; and he marched in the night after the action was over.

This movement of the Marshal's rendered necessary a corresponding one on my part; and I retired from the farm of Quatre Bras upon Genappe, and thence upon Waterloo the next morning, the 17th, at ten o'clock.

The enemy made no effort to pursue Marshal Blucher. On the contrary, a patrole which I sent to Sombref, in the morning, found all quiet, and the enemy's videttes fell back as the patrole advanced. Neither did he attempt to molest our march to the rear, although made in the middle of the day, excepting by following with a large body of cavalry, (brought from his right) the cavalry under the Earl of Uxbridge.

This gave Lord Uxbridge an opportunity of charging them with the 1st Life Guards, upon their debouche from the village of Genappe, upon which occasion his lordship has declared himself to be well satisfied with that regiment.

The position which I took up, in front of Waterloo, crossed the high roads from Charleroi and Nivelle, and had its right thrown back to a ravine near Merke Braine, which was occupied, and its left extended to a height above the hamlet Ter la Haye, which was likewise occupied. In front of the right centre, and near the Nivelle road, we occupied the house and garden of Hougoumont, which covered the return of that flank; and in front of the left centre, we occupied the farm of La Haye Sainte. By our left we communicated with Marshal Prince Blucher, at Wavre, through

Ohaim; and the Marshal had promised me, that in case we should be attacked, he would support me with one or more corps, as might be necessary.

The enemy collected his army, with the exception of the third corps, which had been sent to observe Marshal Blucher, on a range of heights in our front, in the course of the night of the 17th and yesterday morning; and at about ten o'clock he commenced a furious attack upon our post at Hougoumont. I had occupied that post with a detachment from General Byng's brigade of Guards, which was in position in its rear; and it was for some time under the command of Lieutenant-Colonel Macdonald, and afterwards of Colonel Home; and I am happy to add, that it was maintained, throughout the day, with the utmost gallantry by these brave troops, notwithstanding the repeated efforts of large bodies of the enemy to obtain possession of it.

This attack upon the right of our centre was accompanied by a very heavy cannonade upon our whole line, which was destined to support the repeated attacks of cavalry and infantry occasionally mixed, but sometimes separate, which were made upon it. In one of these, the enemy carried the farm-house of La Haye Sainte, as the detachment of the light battalion of the legion which occupied it had expended all its ammunition, and the enemy occupied the only communication there was with them.

The enemy repeatedly charged our infantry with his cavalry; but these attacks were uniformly unsuccessful, and they afforded opportunities to our cavalry to charge, in one of which Lord E. Somerset's brigade, Royal Horse Guards, and 1st Dragoon Guards, highly distinguished themselves; as did that of Major General Sir W. Ponsonby, having taken many prisoners and an eagle.

These attacks were repeated till about seven in the evening, when the enemy made a desperate effort with the cavalry and infantry, to force our left centre, near the farm of La Haye Sainte, which, after a severe contest, was defeated; and having observed that the troops retired from the attack in great confusion, and that the march of General Bulow's corps by Frichermont upon Planchenoit and La Belle Alliance, had begun to take effect; and as I could perceive the fire of his cannon, and as Marshal Prince Blucher had joined in person, with a corps of his army to the left of our line by Ohain, I determined to attack the enemy, and immediately advanced the whole line of infantry, supported by the cavalry and artillery. The attack succeeded in every point; the enemy was forced from his position on the heights, and fled in the utmost confusion, leaving behind him, as far as

I could judge, ONE HUNDRED AND FIFTY PIECES OF CANNON, with their ammunition, which fell into our hands.

I continued the pursuit till long after dark, and then discontinued it, only on account of the fatigue of our troops, who had been engaged during twelve hours, and because I found myself on the same road with Marshal Blucher, who assured me of his intention to follow the enemy throughout the night: he has sent me word this morning, that he had taken sixty pieces of cannon belonging to the Imperial Guard, and several carriages, baggage, &c. belonging to Bonaparte, in Genappe.

I propose to move this morning upon Nivelles, and not to discontinue my operations.

Your lordship will observe, that such a desperate action could not be fought, and such advantages could not be gained, without great loss; and, I am sorry to add, that our's has been immense. In Lieutenant-General Sir Thomas Picton, his Majesty has sustained the loss of an officer who has frequently distinguished himself in his service; and he fell, gloriously leading his division to a charge with bayonets, by which one of the most serious attacks made by the enemy on our position, was defeated.

The Earl of Uxbridge, after having successfully got through this arduous day, received a wound, by almost the last shot fired, which will, I am afraid, deprive his Majesty for some time of his services.

His Royal Highness the Prince of Orange distinguished himself by his gallantry and conduct till he received a wound from a musket-ball, through the shoulder, which obliged him to quit the field.

It gives me the greatest satisfaction to assure your lordship, that the army never, upon any occasion, conducted itself better. The division of Guards, under Lieutenant-General Cooke, who is severely wounded, Major-General Maitland and Major Byng, set an example which was followed by all; and there is no officer, nor description of troops, that did not behave well.

I must, however, particularly mention, for his Royal Highness's approbation, Lieutenant-General Sir H. Clinton, Major-General Adam, Lieutenant-General Charles Baron Alten, severely wounded; Major-General Sir Colin Halket, severely wounded; Colonel Ompteda, Colonel Mitchael, commanding a brigade of the 4th division; Major-Generals Sir James Kempt and Sir Denis Pack, Major-General Lambert, Major-General Lord E. Somerset, Major-General Sir W. Ponsonby, Major-General Sir C. Grant, and Major-General Sir H. Vivian; Major-General Sir O. Vandeleur; Major-General Count Dornberg. I am also particularly indebted to General Lord Hill for his assistance and conduct upon this, as upon all former occasions.

The artillery and engineer departments were conducted much to my satisfaction by Colonel Sir G. Wood, and Colonel Smyth; and I had every reason to be satisfied with the conduct of the Adjutant-General Major-General Barnes, who was wounded, and of the Quarter-Master-General, Colonel Delancy, who was killed by a cannon-shot in the middle of the action. This officer is a serious loss to his Majesty's service, and to me at this moment. I was likewise much indebted to the assistance of Lieutenant-Colonel Lord Fitzroy Somerset, who was severely wounded, and of the officers composing my personal staff, who have suffered severely in this action. Lieutenant-Colonel the Honourable Sir Alexander Gordon, who has died of his wounds, was a most promising officer, and is a serious loss to his Majesty's service.

General Kruse, of the Nassau service, likewise conducted himself much to my satisfaction, as did General Trip, commanding the heavy brigade of cavalry, and General Vanhope, commanding a brigade of infantry of the King of the Netherlands.

General Pozzo di Borgo, General Baron Vincent, General Muffling, and General Alava, were in the field during the action, and rendered me every assistance in their power. Baron Vincent is wounded, but I hope not severely ; and General Pozzo di Borgo received a contusion.

I should not do justice to my feelings, or to Marshal Blucher and the Prussian army, if I did not attribute the successful result of this arduous day to the cordial and timely assistance received from them.

The operation of General Bulow upon the enemy's flank was a most decisive one ; and, even if I had not found myself in a situation to make the attack, which produced the final result, it would have forced the enemy to retire, if his attacks should have failed, and would have prevented him from taking advantage of them, if they should unfortunately have succeeded.

I send, with this dispatch, two eagles, taken by the troops in this action, which Major Percy will have the honour of laying at the feet of his Royal Highness—I beg leave to recommend him to your lordship's protection.

    I have the honour, &c.
     (Signed) WELLINGTON.

MARSHAL BLUCHER'S OFFICIAL REPORT OF THE OPERATIONS OF THE PRUSSIAN ARMY OF THE LOWER RHINE.

It was on the 15th of this month, that Napoleon, after having collected, on the 14th, five corps of his army, and the several corps of the guard, between Maubeuge and Beaumont, commenced hostilities. The points of concentration of the four Prussian corps, were Fleurus, Namur, Ciney, and Hannut; the situation of which made it possible to unite the army, in one of these points, in 24 hours.

On the 15th, Napoleon advanced by Thuin, upon the two banks of the Sambre, against Charleroi. General Ziethen had collected the first corps near Fleurus, and, had, on that day, a very warm action with the enemy, who, after having taken Charleroi, directed his march upon Fleurus. General Ziethen maintained himself in his position near that place.

Field Marshal Blucher intending to fight a great battle with the enemy as soon as possible, the three other corps of the Prussian army were consequently directed upon Sombref, a league and a half from Fleurus, where the 2d and 3d corps were to arrive on the 15th, and the 4th corps on the 16th.

Lord Wellington had united his army between Ath and Nivelles, which enabled him to assist Field Marshal Blucher, in case the battle should be fought on the 15th.

JUNE 16.---BATTLE OF LIGNY.

The Prussian army was posted on the heights between Brie and Sombref, and beyond the last place, and occupied with a large force the villages of St. Amand and Ligny, situate in its front. Mean time, only three corps of the army had joined; the fourth, which was stationed between Liege and Hannut, has been delayed in its march by several circumstances, and was not yet come up. Nevertheless, Field Marshal Blucher resolved to give battle; Lord Wellington having already put in motion, to support him, a strong division of his army, as well as his whole reserve, stationed in the environs of Brussels, and the fourth corps of the Prussian army being also on the point of arriving.

The battle began at three o'clock in the afternoon. The enemy brought up above 130,000 men. The Prussian army was 80,000 strong. The village of St. Amand was the first point attacked by the enemy, who carried it, after a vigorous resistance.

He then directed his efforts against Ligny. It is a large village, solidly built, situate on a rivulet of the same name. It was there that a contest began which may be considered as one of the most obstinate recorded in history. Villages have often been taken and retaken: but here the combat continued for five hours in the villages themselves, and the movements, forwards or backwards, were confined to a very narrow space. On both sides fresh troops continually came up. Each army had, behind the part of the village which it occupied, great masses of infantry, which maintained the combat, and were continually renewed by the reinforcements which they received from their rear, as well as from the heights on the right and left. About two hundred cannon were directed from both sides against the village, which was on fire in several places at once. From time to time the combat extended through the whole line, the enemy having also directed numerous troops against the third corps; however, the main contest was near Ligny. Things seemed to take a favourable turn for the Prussian troops, a part of the village of St. Amand having been retaken by a battalion commanded by the Field Marshal in person; in consequence of which advantage we had regained a height, which had been abandoned after the loss of St. Amand. Nevertheless, the battle continued about Ligny with the same fury. The issue seemed to depend on the arrival of the English troops, or on that of the fourth corps of the Prussian army; in fact, the arrival of this last division would have afforded the Field Marshal the means of making, immediately, with the right wing, an attack, from which great success might be expected: but news arrived that the English division destined to support us, was violently attacked by a corps of the French army, and that it was with great difficulty it had maintained itself in its position at Quatre Bras. The fourth corps of the army did not appear, so that we were forced to maintain, alone, the contest with an army greatly superior in numbers. The evening was already much advanced, and the combat about Ligny continued with the same fury, and the same equality of success; we invoked, but in vain, the arrival of those succours which were so necessary; the danger became every hour more and more urgent; all the divisions were engaged, or had already been so, and there was not any corps at hand able to support them. Suddenly, a division of the enemy's infantry, which, by favour of the night, had made a circuit round the village without being observed, at the same time that some regiments of cuirassiers had forced the passage on the other side, took, in the rear, the main body of our army, which was posted behind the houses. This surprise, on the part of the enemy, was decisive, especially at the moment when our cavalry, also posted on a height behind the village, was repulsed by the enemy's cavalry in repeated attacks.

Our infantry, posted behind Ligny, though forced to retreat, did not suffer itself to be discouraged, either by being surprised by the enemy in the darkness, a circumstance which exaggerates in the mind of man the dangers to which he finds himself exposed, or, by the idea of seeing itself surrounded on all sides. Formed in masses, it coolly repulsed all the attacks of the cavalry, and retreated in good order upon the heights, whence it continued its retrograde movement upon Tilly. In consequence of the sudden irruption of the enemy's cavalry, several of our cannons, in their precipitate retreat, had taken directions which led them to defiles, in which they necessarily fell into disorder; in this manner, 15 pieces fell into the hands of the enemy. At the distance of a quarter of a league from the field of battle, the army formed again. The enemy did not venture to pursue it. The village of Bric remained in our possession during the night, as well as Sombref, where General Thielman had fought with the third corps, and whence he, at day-break, slowly began to retreat towards Gembloux, where the fourth corps, under General Bulow, had at length arrived during the night. The first and second corps proceeded in the morning behind the defile of Mount St. Guibert. Our loss in killed and wounded was great; the enemy, however, took from us no prisoners, except a part of our wounded. The battle was lost, but not our honour. Our soldiers had fought with a bravery which equalled every expectation; their fortitude remained unshaken, because every one retained his confidence in his own strength. On this day, Field Marshal Blucher had encountered the greatest dangers. A charge of cavalry, led on by himself, had failed. While that of the enemy was vigorously pursuing, a musket shot struck the Field Marshal's horse: the animal, far from being stopped in his career by this wound, began to gallop more furiously till it dropped down dead. The Field Marshal, stunned by the violent fall, lay entangled under the horse. The enemy's cuirassiers, following up their advantage, advanced: our last horseman had already passed by the Field Marshal, an Adjutant alone remained with him, and had just alighted, resolved to share his fate. The danger was great, but Heaven watched over us. The enemy, pursuing their charge, passed rapidly by the Field Marshal without seeing him: the next moment, a second charge of our cavalry having repulsed them, they again passed by him with the same precipitation, not perceiving him, any more than they had done the first time. Then, but not without difficulty, the Field Marshal was disengaged from under the dead horse, and he immediately mounted a dragoon horse.

On the 17th, in the evening, the Prussian army concentrated itself in the environs of Wavre. Napoleon put himself in motion against Lord Wellington upon the great road leading from Charleroi to Brussels. An English division maintained on the same day, near Quatre Bras, a very severe contest with the enemy. Lord Wellington had taken a position on the road to Brussels, having his right wing leaning upon Braine-la-Len, the centre near Mount St. Jean, and the left wing against La Haye Sainte. Lord Wellington wrote to the Field Marshal, that he was resolved to accept the battle in this position, if the Field Marshal would support him with two corps of his army. The Field Marshal promised to come with his whole army; he even proposed, in case Napoleon should not attack, that the Allies themselves, with their whole united force, should attack him the next day. This may serve to show how little the battle of the 16th had disorganized the Prussian army, or weakened its moral strength. Thus ended the day of the 17th.

BATTLE OF THE 18th.

At break of day the Prussian army again began to move. The 4th and 2d corps marched by St. Lambert, where they were to take a position, covered by the forest, near Frichemont, to take the enemy in the rear, when the moment should appear favourable. The first corps was to operate by Ohain, on the right flank of the enemy. The third corps was to follow slowly, in order to afford succour in case of need. The battle began about 10 o'clock in the morning. The English army occupied the heights of Mount St. Jean; that of the French was on the heights before Planchenoit: the former was about 80,000 strong; the enemy had above 130,000. In a short time, the battle became general along the whole line. It seems that Napoleon had the design to throw the left wing upon the centre, and thus to effect the separation of the English army from the Prussian, which he believed to be retreating upon Maestricht. For this purpose, he had placed the greatest part of his reserve in the centre, against his right wing, and upon this point he attacked with fury. The English army fought with a valour which it is impossible to surpass. The repeated charges of the Old Guard were baffled by the intrepidity of the Scottish regiments; and at every charge the French cavalry was overthrown by the English cavalry. But the superiority of the enemy in numbers was too great; Napoleon continually brought forward considerable masses, and, with whatever firmness the English troops maintained themselves in their position, it was not possible but that such heroic exertions must have a limit.

It was half-past four o'clock. The excessive difficulties of the passage by the defile of St. Lambert, had considerably retarded the march of the Prussian columns, so that only two brigades of the fourth corps had arrived at the covered position which was assigned to them. The decisive moment was come; there was not an instant to be lost. The Generals did not suffer it to escape. They resolved immediately to begin the attack with the troops which they had at hand. General Bulow, therefore, with two brigades and a corps of cavalry, advanced rapidly upon the rear of the enemy's right wing. The enemy did not lose his presence of mind; he instantly turned his reserve against us, and a murderous conflict began on that side. The combat remained long uncertain, while the battle with the English army still continued with the same violence.

Towards six o'clock in the evening, we received the news that General Thielman, with the third corps, was attacked near Wavre by a very considerable corps of the enemy, and that they were already disputing the possession of the town. The Field Marshal, however, did not suffer himself to be disturbed by this news; it was on the spot where he was, and no where else, that the affair was to be decided. A conflict continually supported by the

BATTLE OF WATERLOO. 159

same obstinacy, and kept up by fresh troops, could alone insure the victory, and if it were obtained here, any reverse sustained near Wavre was of little consequence. The columns, therefore, continued their movements. It was half an hour past seven, and the issue of the battle was still uncertain. The whole of the 4th corps, and a part of the 2d, under General Pirch, had successively come up. The French troops fought with desperate fury: however, some uncertainty was perceived in their movements, and it was observed that some pieces of cannon were retreating. At this moment, the first columns of the corps of General Ziethen arrived on the points of attack, near the village of Smonhen, on the enemy's right flank, and instantly charged. This moment decided the defeat of the enemy. His right wing was broken in three places; he abandoned his positions. Our troops rushed forward at the *pas de charge*, and attacked him on all sides, while at the same time, the whole English line advanced.

Circumstances were extremely favourable to the attack formed by the Prussian army: the ground rose in an amphitheatre, so that our artillery could freely open its fire from the summit of a great many heights which rose gradually above each other, and in the intervals of which the troops descended into the plain, formed into brigades, and in the greatest order; while fresh troops continually unfolded themselves, issuing from the forest on the height behind us. The enemy, however, still preserved means to retreat, till the village of Planchenoit, which he had on his rear, and which was defended by the guard, was, after several bloody attacks, carried by storm. From that time the retreat became a rout, which soon spread throughout the whole French army, which, in its dreadful confusion, hurrying away every thing that attempted to stop it, soon assumed the appearance of the flight of an army of barbarians. It was half-past nine. The Field Marshal assembled all the superior officers, and gave orders to send the last horse and the last man in pursuit of the enemy. The van of the army accelerated its march. The French being pursued without intermission, was absolutely disorganised. The causeway presented the appearance of an immense shipwreck; it was covered with an innumerable quantity of cannon, caissons, carriages, baggage, arms, and wrecks of every kind. Those of the enemy who had attempted to repose for a time, and had not expected to be so quickly pursued, were driven from more than nine bivouacs. In some villages they attempted to maintain themselves; but as soon as they heard the beating of our drums, or the sound of the trumpet, they either fled or threw themselves into the houses, where they were cut down or made prisoners. It was moonlight, which greatly favoured the pursuit, for the whole march was but a continued chace, either in the corn fields or the houses.

At Genappe, the enemy had entrenched himself with cannon, and overturned carriages: at our approach, we suddenly heard in the town a great noise and a motion of carriages; at the entrance we were exposed to a brisk fire of musketry; we replied by some cannon shot, followed by a *hurrah*, and an instant after, the town was ours. It was here that, among many other equipages, the carriage of Napoleon was taken; he had just left it to mount on horseback, and, in his hurry, had forgotten in it his sword and hat. Thus the affairs continued till break of day. About 40,000 men, in the most complete disorder, the remains of the whole army, have saved themselves retreating through Charleroi, partly without arms, and carrying with them only 27 pieces of their numerous artillery.

The enemy, in his flight, had passed all his fortresses, the only defence of his frontiers, which are now passed by our armies.

BATTLE OF WATERLOO.

At three o'clock, Napoleon had dispatched, from the field of battle, a courier to Paris, with the news that victory was no longer doubtful: a few hours after, he had no longer any army left. We have not yet any exact account of the enemy's loss; it is enough to know, that two-thirds of the whole were killed, wounded, or prisoners: among the latter are Generals Monton, Duhesme, and Compans. Up to this time about 500 cannon, and above 500 caissons, are in our hands.

Few victories have been so complete; and there is certainly no example that an army, two days after losing a battle, engaged in such an action, and so gloriously maintained it. Honour be to troops capable of so much firmness and valour! In the middle of the position occupied by the French army, and exactly upon the height, is a farm called *La Belle Alliance*. The march of all the Prussian columns was directed towards this farm, which was visible from every side. It was there that Napoleon was during the battle; it was thence that he gave his orders, that he flattered himself with the hopes of victory; and it was there that his ruin was decided. There, too, it was, that, by a happy chance, Field Marshal Blucher and Lord Wellington met in the dark, and mutually saluted each other as victors.

In commemoration of the alliance which now subsists between the English and Prussian nations, of the union of the two armies, and their reciprocal confidence, the Field Marshall desired, that this battle should bear the name of *La Belle Alliance*.

By the order of Field Marshal Blucher,

General GNEISENAU.

SPANISH ACCOUNT.

The following is a copy of a dispatch from General Miguel Alava, Minister Plenipotentiary to the King of the Netherlands from the King of Spain, to Don Pedro Cevallos, Principal Secretary of State to Ferdinand VII.

(TRANSLATED FROM THE SPANISH.)

Supplement to the Madrid Gazette of Thursday, 13th *July*, 1815.

Lieutenant-General of the Royal Armies, Don Miguel de Alava, Minister Plenipotentiary of His Excellency Don Pedro Cevallos, First Secretary of State, the following letter:

Most Excellent Sir,

The short space of time that has intervened between the departure of the last post and the victory of the 18th, has not allowed me to write to your Excellency so diffusely as I could have wished; and although the army is, at this moment, on the point of marching, and I also am going to set out for the Hague to deliver my credentials, which I did not receive till this morning; nevertheless, I will give your Excellency some details respecting this important event, which, possibly, may bring us to the end of the war much sooner than we had any reason to expect.

I informed your Excellency, under date of the 16th inst. that Bonaparte, marching from Maubeuge and Philippeville, had attacked the Prussian posts on the Sambre, and that, after driving them from Charleroi, he had entered that city on the 15th.

On the 16th, the Duke of Wellington ordered his army to assemble on the point of Quatre Bras, where the roads cross from Namur to Nivelle, and from Brussels to Charleroi; and he himself proceeded to the same point, at seven in the morning.

On his arrival, he found the Hereditary Prince of Orange, with a division of his own army, holding the enemy in check, till the other divisions of the army were collected.

By this time, the British division, under General Picton, had arrived, with which the Duke kept up an unequal contest with more than 30,000 of the enemy, without losing an inch of ground. The British Guards, several regiments of infantry, and the Scottish Brigade, covered themselves with glory on this day; and Lord Wellington told me, on the following day, that he never saw his troops behave better, during the number of years he had commanded them.

The French Cuirassiers likewise suffered much on their part; for, confiding in their breast-plates, they approached the British squares so near, that they killed officers of the 42d regiment with their swords; but those valiant men, without flinching, kept up so strong a fire, that the whole ground was covered with the Cuirassiers and their horses.

In the meantime, the troops kept coming up; and the night put an end to the contest in this quarter.

During this time, Bonaparte was fighting, with the remainder of his forces, against Marshal Blucher, with whom he had commenced a bloody action at five in the afternoon; from which time, till nine in the evening, he was constantly repulsed by the Prussians, with great loss on both sides. But, at that moment, he made his cavalry charge with so much vigour, that they broke the Prussian line of infantry, and introduced disorder and confusion throughout.

Whether it was that Bonaparte did not perceive this incident, or that he had experienced a great loss; or, what is more probable, that Marshal Blucher had re-established the battle, the fact is, that he derived no advantage whatever from this accident, and that he left him quiet during the whole of the night of the 16th.

Lord Wellington, who, by the morning of the 17th, had collected the whole of his army in the position of Quatre Bras, was combining his measures to attack the enemy, when he received a dispatch from Marshal Blucher, participating to him the events of the preceding day, together with the incident that had snatched the victory out of his hands; adding, that the loss he had experienced was of such a nature, that he was forced to retreat to Wavre, on our left, where the corps of Bulow would unite with him, and that on the 19th he would be ready for any thing he might wish to undertake.

In consequence of this, Lord Wellington was obliged immediately to retreat, and this he effected in such a manner, that the enemy did not dare to interrupt him in it. He took up a position on Braine-le-Leud, in front of the great wood of Soignés, as he had previously determined, and placed his head quarters in Waterloo.

I joined the army on that morning, though I had received no orders to that effect, because I believed that I should thus best serve his Majesty, and at the same time fulfil your Excellency's directions; and this determination has afforded me the satisfaction of having been present at the most important battle that has been fought for many centuries, in its consequences, its duration, and the talents of the chiefs who commanded on both sides, and because the peace of the world, and the future security of all Europe, may be said to have depended on its result.

The position occupied by his lordship was very good; but towards the centre, it had various weak points, which required good troops to guard them, and much science and skill on the part of the general in chief. These qualifications were, however, to be found in abundance in the British troops and their illustrious commander; and, it may be asserted, without offence to any one, that to them both belongs the chief part, or all the glory of this memorable day.

On the right of the position, and a little in advance, was a country house, the importance of which Lord Wellington quickly perceived, because, without it, the position could not be attacked on that side, and it might therefore be considered as its key.

The Duke confided this important point to three companies of the English guards under the command of Lord Saltoun, and laboured, during the night of the 17th, in fortifying it as well as possible, covering its garden, and a wood which served as its park, with Nassau troops, as sharp-shooters.

At half past ten, a movement was observed in the enemy's line, and many officers were seen coming from and going to a particular point, where there was a very considerable corps of infantry, which we afterwards understood to be the Imperial guard; here was Bonaparte in person, and from this point issued all the orders. In the mean time, the enemy's masses were forming, and every thing announced the approaching combat, which began at half past eleven, the enemy attacking desperately with one of his corps, and, with his usual shouts, the country-house on the right.

The Nassau troops found it necessary to abandon their post; but the enemy met such resistance in the house, that, though they surrounded it on three sides, and attacked it most desperately, they were compelled to desist from their enterprise, leaving a great number of killed and wounded on the spot. Lord Wellington sent fresh English troops, who recovered the wood and garden, and the combat ceased, for the present, on this side.

The enemy then opened a horrible fire of artillery from more than 200 pieces, under cover of which Bonaparte made a general attack, from the centre to the right, with infantry and cavalry, in such numbers, that it required all the skill of his lordship to post his troops, and all the good qualities of the latter, to resist the attack.

General Picton, who was with his division on the road from Brussels to Charleroi, advanced with the bayonet to receive them; but was unfortunately killed at the moment when the enemy, appalled by the attitude of this division, fired, and then fled.

The English life Guards then charged with the greatest vigour, and the 49th and 105th French regiments lost their respective eagles in this charge, together with from 2 to 3000 prisoners. A column of cavalry, at whose head were the cuirassiers, advanced to charge the life guards, and thus save their infantry, but the guards received them with the greatest valour, and the most sanguinary cavalry fight, perhaps, ever witnessed, was the consequence.

The French cuirassiers were completely beaten, in spite of their cuirasses, by troops who had nothing of the sort, and lost one of their eagles in this conflict, which was taken by the heavy English cavalry, called the *Royals*.

About this time, accounts came that the Prussian corps of Bulow had arrived at St. Lambert, and that Prince Blucher, with the other, under the command of general Thielman (Ziethen) was advancing, with all haste, to take part in the combat, leaving the other two in Wavre, which had suffered so much in the battle of the 16th, in Fleurus. The arrival of these troops was so much the more necessary, in consequence of the forces of the enemy being more than triple, and our loss having been horrid during an unequal combat, from half past eleven in the morning, till five in the afternoon.

Bonaparte, who did not believe them to be so near, and who reckoned upon destroying Lord Wellington before their arrival, perceived that he had fruitlessly lost more than five hours, and that in the critical position in which he would soon be placed, there remained no other resource but that of desperately attacking the weak part of the English position, and thus, if possible, beat the Duke before his right was turned and attacked by the Prussians.

Henceforward, therefore, the whole was a repetition of attacks by cavalry and infantry, supported by more than 300 pieces of artillery, which unfortunately made horrible ravages in our line, and killed and wounded officers, artillerists, and horses, in the weakest part of the position.

The enemy, aware of this destruction, made a charge with the whole cavalry of his guard, which took some pieces of cannon that could not be withdrawn; but the Duke, who was at this point, charged them with three battalions of English and three of Brunswickers, and compelled them in a moment to abandon the artillery, though we were unable to withdraw them for want of horses; nor did they dare to advance to recover them.

At last, about seven in the evening, Bonaparte made a last effort, and putting himself at the head of his guards, attacked the above point of the English position with such vigour, that he drove back the Brunswickers who occupied part of it; and, for a moment, the victory was undecided, and even more than doubtful.

The Duke, who felt that the moment was most critical, spoke to the Brunswick troops with that ascendancy which every great man possesses, made them return to the charge, and, putting himself at their head, again restored the combat, exposing himself to every kind of personal danger.

Fortunately, at this moment, he perceived the fire of Marshal Blucher, who was attacking the enemy's right with his usual impetuosity; and the moment of decisive attack being come, the Duke put himself at the head of the English Foot-Guards, spoke a few words to them, which were replied to by a general *hurrah*, and his Grace himself leading them on with his hat, they marched at the point of the bayonet, to come to close action with the Imperial Guard. But the latter began a retreat, which was soon converted into flight, and the most complete rout ever witnessed by military men. Entire columns, throwing down their arms and cartouch-boxes, in order to escape the better, abandoned the spot on which they had been formed, where we took possession of 150 pieces of cannon. The rout at Vittoria was not comparable to this, and it only resembles it, inasmuch as on both occasions, they lost all the train of artillery and stores of the army, as well as all the baggage.

The Duke followed the enemy as far as Genappe, where he found the respectable Blucher, and both embraced in the most cordial manner, on the royal road of Charleroi; but finding himself in the same point as the Prussians, and that his army stood in need of rest after so dreadful a struggle, he left to Blucher the charge of following up the enemy, who swore that he would not leave them a moment of rest. This he is now doing, and yesterday, at noon, he had reached Charleroi, from whence at night, he intended to proceed on after them.

This is, in substance, what has happened on this memorable day; but the consequences of this event are too visible for me to detain myself in stating them.

Bonaparte, now tottering on his usurped throne, without money and without troops to recruit his armies, has received so mortal a blow, that, according to the report of the prisoners, no other resource is left him, " than to cut his own throat."

For this reason, they say, they never saw him expose his person so much, and that he seemed to seek death, in order not to survive a defeat fraught with such fatal consequences to him.

I told your Excellency, under date of the 16th, that his manœuvre appeared to me extremely daring before such generals as Blucher and the Duke; the event has fully justified my prediction. For this reason, I conceive, that his executing it has arisen from nothing else than desperation, at the appearance of the enormous troops about to attack him on all quarters of France, and in order to give one of his customary blows before the Russians and Austrians came up.

His military reputation is lost for ever, and, on this occasion, there is no treason on the part of the Allies, nor bridges blown up before their time, on which to throw the blame; all the shame will fall upon himself.

Numerical superiority, superiority of artillery, all was in his favour; and his having commenced the attack, proves that he had sufficient means to execute it.

In short, this talisman, which, like a charm, had enchanted French military men, has been dashed to pieces on this occasion. Bonaparte has for ever lost his reputation of being invincible; and, henceforward, this reputation will be preserved by an honourable man, who, far from employing this glorious title in disturbing and enslaving Europe, will convert it into an instrument of her felicity, and in procuring for her that peace she so much requires.

The loss of the British is horrid, and of those who were by the side of the Duke, he and myself alone, remained untouched in our persons and horses.

The Duke of Brunswick was killed on the 16th, and the Prince of Orange and his cousin, the Prince of Nassau, aidde-camp to the Duke of Wellington, received two balls. The Prince of Orange distinguished himself extremely; but, unfortunately, although his wound is not dangerous, it will deprive the army of his important services for some time, and possibly he may lose the use of his left arm.

Lord Uxbridge, general of cavalry, received a wound at the close of the action, which made the amputation of his right leg necessary; an irreparable loss, for it would be difficult to find another chief to lead on the cavalry, with the same courage and skill.

The Duke was unable to refrain from sheding tears, on witnessing the death of so many brave and honourable men, and the loss of so many friends and faithful companions, and nothing but the importance of the triumph can compensate so considerable a loss.

This morning he has proceeded on to Nivelles, and tomorrow he will advance to Mons, from whence he will immediately enter France. The opportunity cannot be better.

I cannot close this dispatch without stating to your Excellency, for the information of his Majesty, that Capt. Don Nicholas de Minuissir, of Doyle's regiment, and of whom I before spoke to your Excellency, as well as of his destination in the army, conducted himself yesterday with the greatest valour and steadiness, having been wounded when the Nassau troops were driven from the garden, he rallied them and made them return to their post. During the action, he had a horse wounded under him, and by his former conduct, as well as by that of this day, he is worthy of receiving from his Majesty a proof of his satisfaction.

This officer is well known in the war-office, as well as to Gen. Don Josef de Zayas, who has duly appreciated his merits.

God preserve your Excellency many years, &c. &c.
(Signed) MIGUEL de ALAVA.
Brussels, 20th of June, 1815.
To his Excellency, Don Pedro Cevallos, &c. &c.

P. S. The number of prisoners cannot be stated, for they are bringing in great numbers every moment. There are many generals among the prisoners; among whom are the Count de Lobau, aid-de-camp to Bonaparte, and Cambrone, who accompanied him to Elba.

FRENCH OFFICIAL DETAIL OF THE BATTLES WITH THE PRUSSIANS AND ENGLISH, WITH NEY'S OBSERVATIONS.

BATTLE OF LIGNY-UNDER-FLEURUS.

Paris, June 21.

On the morning of the 16th the army occupied the following position:

The left wing, commanded by the Marshal Duke of Elchingen, and consisting of the 1st and 2d corps of infantry, and the 2d of cavalry, occupied the positions of Frasne.

The right wing, commanded by Marshal Grouchy, and composed of the 3d and 4th corps of infantry, and the 3d corps of cavalry, occupied the heights in rear of Fleurus.

The Emperor's head-quarters were at Charleroi, where were the Imperial Guard and the 6th corps.

The left wing had orders to march upon Quatre Bras, and the right upon Sombref. The Emperor advanced to Fleurus with his reserve.

The columns of Marshal Grouchy being in march, perceived, after having passed Fleurus, the enemy's army, commanded by Field Marshal Blucher, occupying with its left the heights of the mill of Bussy, the village of Sombref, and extending its cavalry a great way forward on the road to Namur; its right was at St. Amand, and occupied that large village in great force, having before it a ravine which formed its position.

The Emperor reconnoitred the strength and the positions of the enemy, and resolved to attack immediately. It became necessary to change front, the right in advance, and pivoting upon Fleurus.

General Vandamme marched upon St. Amand, General Gerard upon Ligny, and Marshal Grouchy upon Sombref. The 4th division of the 2d corps, commanded by General Girard, marched in reserve behind the corps of General Vandamme. The guard was drawn up on the heights of Fleurus, as well as the cuirassiers of General Milhaud.

At three in the afternoon, these dispositions were finished. The division of General Lefol, forming part of the corps of General Vandamme, was first engaged, and made itself master of St. Amand, whence it drove out the enemy at the point of the bayonet. It kept its ground during the whole of the engagement, at the burial-ground and steeple of St. Amand; but that village, which is very extensive, was the theatre of various combats during the evening; the whole corps of General Vandamme was there engaged, and the enemy there fought in considerable force.

BATTLE OF WATERLOO. 173

General Girard, placed as a reserve to the corps of General Vandamme, turned the village by its right, and fought there with its accustomed valour. The respective forces were supported on both sides by about 50 pieces of cannon each.

On the right, General Girard came into action with the 4th corps, at the village of Ligny, which was taken and retaken several times.

Marshal Grouchy, on the extreme right, and General Pajol fought at the village of Sombref. The enemy showed from 80 to 90,000 men, and a great number of cannon.

At seven o'clock we were masters of all the villages situate on the bank of the ravine, which covered the enemy's position; but he still occupied, with all his masses, the heights of the mill of Bussy.

The Emperor returned with his guard to the village of Ligny; General Girard directed General Pecheux to debouch with what remained of the reserve, almost all the trroops having been engaged in that village.

Eight battalions of the guard debouched with fixed bayonets, and behind them, four squadrons of the guards, the cuirassiers of general Delort, those of General Milhaud, and the grenadiers of the horse guards. The old guard attacked with the bayonet the enemy's columns, which were on the heights of Bussy, and in an instant covered the field of battle with dead. The squadron of the guard attacked and broke a square, and the cuirassiers repulsed the enemy in all directions. At half past nine o'clock we had forty pieces of cannon, several carriages, colours, and prisoners, and the enemy sought safety in a precipitate retreat. At ten o'clock the battle was finished, and we found ourselves masters of the field of battle.

General Lutzow, a partizan, was taken prisoner. The prisoners assure us, that Field Marshal Blucher was wound-

3

ed. The flower of the Prussian army was destroyed in this battle. Its loss could not be less than 15,000 men. Ours was 3000 killed and wounded.

On the left, Marshal Ney had marched on Quatre Bras with a division, which cut in pieces an English division which was stationed there; but being attacked by the Prince of Orange with 25,000 men, partly English, partly Hanoverians in the pay of England, he retired upon his position at Frasne. There a multiplicity of combats took place; the enemy obstinately endeavoured to force it, but in vain. The Duke of Elchingen waited for the 1st corps, which did not arrive till night; he confined himself to maintaining his position. In a square attacked by the 8th regiment of cuirassiers, the colours of the 69th regiment of English infantry fell into our hands. The Duke of Brunswick was killed. The Prince of Orange has been wounded. We are assured that the enemy had many personages and generals of note killed or wounded; we estimated the loss of the English at from 4 to 5000 men; ours on this side was very considerable, it amounts to 4200 killed or wounded. The combat ended with the approach of night. Lord Wellington then evacuated Quatre Bras, and proceeded to Genappe.

In the morning of the 17th, the Emperor repaired to Quatre Bras, whence he marched to attack the English army: he drove it to the entrance of the forest of Soignes with the left wing and the reserve. The right wing advanced by Sombref, in pursuit of Field Marshal Blucher, who was going towards Wavre, where he appeared to wish to take a position.

At ten o'clock in the evening, the English army occupied Mount St. Jean with its centre, and was in position before the forest of Soignes : it would have required three hours to attack it; we were therefore obliged to postpone it till the next day.

The head quarters of the Emperor were established at the farm of Oaillon, near Planchenoit. The rain fell in torrents. Thus, on the 16th, the left wing, the right, and the reserve, were equally engaged, at a distance of about two leagues.

BATTLE OF MOUNT ST. JEAN.

At nine in the morning, the rain having somewhat abated, the 1st corps put itself in motion, and placed itself with the left, on the road to Brussels, and opposite the village of Mount St. Jean, which appeared the centre of the enemy's position. The 2d corps leaned its right upon the road to Brussels, and its left upon a small wood, within cannon shot of the English army. The cuirassiers were in reserve behind, and the guards in reserve upon the heights. The 6th corps, with the cavalry of General D'Aumont, under the order of Count Lobau, was destined to proceed in rear of our right to oppose a Prussian corps, which appeared to have escaped Marshal Grouchy, and to intend to fall upon our right flank, an intention which had been made known to us by our reports, and by the letter of a Prussian general, inclosing an order of battle, and which was taken by our light troops.

The troops were full of ardour. We estimated the force of the English army at 80,000 men. We supposed that the Prussian corps, which might be in line towards the right, might be 15,000 men. The enemy's force, then, was upwards of 90,000 men, ours less numerous.

At noon, all the preparations being terminated, Prince Jerome, commanding a division of the second corps, and destined to form the extreme length of it, advanced upon the wood of which the enemy occupied a part. The cannonade began. The enemy supported, with 30 pieces of cannon, the troops he had sent to keep the wood. We made also on our side dispositions of artillery. At one o'clock, Prince Jerome was master of all the wood, and the whole English army fell back behind a curtain. Count d'Erlon then attacked the village of Mount St. Jean, and supported his attack with 80 pieces of cannon, which must have occasioned great loss to the English army. All the efforts were made towards the ridge. A brigade of the 1st division of Count d'Erlon took the village of Mount St. Jean; a second brigade was charged by a corps of English cavalry, which occasioned it much loss. At the same moment, a division of English cavalry charged the battery of Count d'Erlon by its right, and disorganised several pieces; but the cuirassiers of General Milhaud charged that division, three regiments of which were broken and cut up.

It was three in the afternoon. The Emperor made the guard advance to place it in the plain upon the ground which the first corps had occupied at the outset of the battle; this corps being already in advance. The Prussian division, whose movement had been foreseen, then engaged with the light troops of Count Lobau, spreading its fire upon our whole right flank. It was expedient, before undertaking any thing elsewhere, to wait for the event of this attack. Hence, all the means in reserve were ready to succour Count Lobau, and overwhelm the Prussian corps when it should be advanced.

This done the Emperor had the design of leading an attack upon the village of Mount St. Jean, from which we expected decisive success; but, by a movement of impatience so frequent in our military annals, and, which has often been so fatal to us, the cavalry of reserve having perceived a retrograde movement made by the English to shelter themselves from our batteries, from which they suffered so much, crowned the heights of Mount St. Jean, and charged the infantry. This movement, which, made in time, and supported by the reserves, must have decided the day, made in an isolated manner, and before affairs on the right were terminated, became fatal.

Having no means of countermanding it, the enemy showing many masses of cavalry and infantry, and our two divisions of cuirassiers being engaged, all our cavalry ran at the same moment to support their comrades. There, for three hours, numerous charges were made, which enabled us to penetrate several squares, and to take six standards of the light infantry, an advantage out of proportion with the loss which our cavalry experienced by the grape shot and musket-firing. It was impossible to dispose of our reserves of infantry until we had repulsed the flank attack of the Prussian corps. This attack always prolonged itself perpendicularly upon our right flank. The Emperor sent thither General Duhesme with the young guard, and several batteries of reserve. The enemy was kept in check, repulsed, and fell back—he had exhausted his forces, and we had nothing more to fear. It was this moment that was indicated for an attack upon the centre of the enemy. As the cuirassiers suffered by the grape-shot, we sent four battalions of the middle guard to protect the cuirassiers, keep the position, and, if possible, disengage and draw back into the plain a part of our cavalry.

Two other battalions were sent to keep themselves *en potence* upon the extreme left of the division, which had manoeuvred upon our flanks, in order not to have any uneasiness on that side—the rest was disposed in reserve, part to occupy the *potence* in rear of Mount St. Jean, part upon the ridge in rear of the field of battle, which formed our position of retreat.

In this state of affairs, the battle was gained; we occupied all the positions, which the enemy occupied at the outset of the battle: our cavalry having been too soon and ill employed, we could no longer hope for decisive success; but Marshal Grouchy having learned the movement of the Prussian corps, marched upon the rear of that corps, which insured us a signal success for next day. After eight hours fire and charges of infantry and cavalry, all the army saw with joy the battle gained, and the field of battle in our power.

At half after eight o'clock, the four battalions of the middle guard, who had been sent to the ridge on the other side of Mount St. Jean, in order to support the cuirassiers, being greatly annoyed by the grape shot, endeavoured to carry the batteries with the bayonet. At the end of the day, a charge directed against their flank, by several English squadrons, put them in disorder. The fugitives recrosed the ravine. Several regiments, near at hand, seeing some troops belonging to the guard in confusion, believed it was the old gnard, and in consequence were thrown into disorder. Cries of *all is lost, the guard is driven back*, were heard on every side. The soldiers pretend even that on many points ill-disposed persons cried out, *sauve qui peut*. However this may be, a complete panic at once spread itself throughout the whole field of battle, and they threw themselves in the greatest disorder on the line of communication; soldiers, cannoneers, caissons, all pressed to this point; the old guard, which was in reserve, was infected, and was itself hurried along.

In an instant, the whole army was nothing but a mass of confusion; all the soldiers, of all arms, were mixed *pêle-mêle*, and it was utterly impossible to rally a single corps. The enemy, who perceived this astonishing confusion, immediately attacked with their cavalry, and increased the disorder, and such was the confusion, owing to night coming on, that it was impossible to rally the troops, and point out to them their error. Thus a battle terminated, a day of false manœuvres rectified, the greatest success insured for the next day,—all was lost by a moment of panic terror. Even the squadrons of *service*, drawn up by the side of the Emperor, were overthrown and disorganized by these tumultuous waves, and there was then nothing else to be done but to follow the torrent. The parks of reserve, the baggage which had not repassed the Sambre, in short every thing that was on the field of battle, remained in the power of the enemy. It was impossible to wait for the troops on our right; every one knows what the bravest army in the world is when thus mixed and thrown into confusion, and when its organization no longer exists.

The Emperor crossed the Sambre at Charleroi, at five o'clock in the morning of the 19th. Philippeville and Avesnes have been given as the points of re-union. Prince Jerome, General Morand, and other generals have there already rallied a part of the army. Marshal Grouchy, with the corps on the right, is moving on the Lower Sambre.

The loss of the enemy must have been very great, if we may judge from the number of standards we have taken from them, and from the retrograde movements which he made;—our's cannot be calculated till after the troops shall have been collected. Before the disorder broke out, we had already experienced a very considerable loss, particularly in our cavalry, so fatally, though so bravely engaged. Notwithstanding these losses, this brave cavalry constantly kept the position it had taken from the English, and only abandoned it when the tumult and disorder of the field of battle forced it. In the midst of the night, and the obstacles which encumbered their route, it could not preserve its own organization.

The artillery has, as usual, covered itself with glory. The carriages belonging to the head-quarters remained in their ordinary position : no retrograde movement being judged necessary. In the course of the night they fell into the enemy's hands.

Such has been the issue of the battle of Mount St. Jean, glorious for the French armies, and yet so fatal.

THE PRINCE OF MOSKWA (MARSHAL NEY) TO HIS EXCELLENCY THE DUKE OF OTRANTO.

M. LE DUC,—The most false and defamatory reports have been spreading for some days over the public mind, upon the conduct which I have pursued during this short and unfortunate campaign. The journals have reported those odious calumnies, and appear to lend them credit. After having fought for twenty-five years for my country, after having shed my blood for its glory and independence, an attempt is made to accuse me of treason ; an attempt is made to mark me out to the people, and the army itself, as the author of the disaster it has just experienced.

Forced to break silence, while it is always painful to speak of oneself, and above all, to answer calumnies, I address myself to you, Sir, as the President of the Provisional Government, for the purpose of laying before you a faithful statement of the events I have witnessed. On the 11th of June, I received an order from the Minister of War to repair

BATTLE OF WATERLOO. 181

to the Imperial presence. I had no command, and no information upon the composition and strength of the army. Neither the Emperor nor his Minister had given me any previous hint, from which I could anticipate that I should be employed in the present campaign, I was consequently taken by surprise, without horses, without accoutrements, and without money, and I was obliged to borrow the necessary expenses of my journey. Having arrived on the 12th, at Laon, on the 13th at Avesnes, and on the 14th at Beaumont, I purchased, in this last city, two horses from the Duke of Treviso, with which I repaired, on the 15th, to Charleroi, accompanied by my first aid-de-camp, the only officer who attended me. I arrived at the moment when the enemy, attacked by our troops, was retreating upon Fleurus and Gosselies.

The Emperor ordered me immediately to put myself at the head of the 1st and 2d corps of infantry, commanded by Lieutenant Generals d'Erlon and Reille, of the divisions of light cavalry of Lieutenant General Pine, of the division of light cavalry of the guard under the command of Lieutenant Generals Lefebvre Desnouettes and Colbert, and of two divisions of cavalry of the Count Valmy, forming, in all, eight divisions of infantry, and four of cavalry. With these troops, a part of which only I had as yet under my immediate command, I pursued the enemy, and forced him to evacuate Gosselies, Frasnes, Millet, Heppegnies. There they took up a position for the night, with the exception of the 1st corps, which was still at Marchiennes, and which did not join me till the following day.

On the 16th I received orders to attack the English in their position at Quatre Bras. We advanced towards the enemy with an enthusiasm difficult to be described. Nothing resisted our impetuosity. The battle became general, and victory was no longer doubtful, when, at the moment that I intended to order up the first corps of infantry, which had been left by me in reserve at Frasnes, I learned that the Emperor had disposed of it without adverting me of the circumstance, as well as of the division of Girard of the second corps, on purpose to direct them upon St. Amand, and to strengthen his left wing, which was vigorously engaged with the Prussians. The shock which this intelligence gave me, confounded me. Having no longer under me more than three divisions, instead of the eight upon which I calculated, I was obliged to renounce the hopes of victory; and, in spite of all my efforts, in spite of the intrepidity and devotion of my troops, my utmost efforts after that could only maintain me in my position till the close of the day. About nine o'clock, the first corps was sent me by the Emperor, to whom it had been of no service. Thus twenty-five or thirty thousand men were, I may say, paralized, and were idly paraded during the whole of the battle from the right to the left, and the left to the right, without firing a shot.

It is impossible for me, Sir, not to arrest your attention for a moment upon these details, in order to bring before your view all the consequences of this false movement, and, in general, of the bad arrangements during the whole of the day. By what fatality, for example, did the Emperor, instead of leading all his forces against Lord Wellington, who would have been attacked unawares, and could not have resisted, consider this attack as secondary? How did the Emperor, after the passage of the Sambre, conceive it possible to fight two battles on the same day? It was to oppose forces double ours, and to do what military men who were witnesses of it can scarcely yet comprehend. Instead of this, had he left a corps of observation to watch the Prussians,

BATTLE OF WATERLOO. 133

and marched with his most powerful masses to support me, the English army had undoubtedly been destroyed between Quatre Bras and Genappes; and this position, which separated the two allied armies, being once in our power, would have opened for the Emperor an opportunity of advancing to the right of the Prussians, and of crushing them in their turn. The general opinion in France, and especially in the army, was, that the Emperor would have bent his whole efforts to annihilate first the English army; and circumstances were favourable for the accomplishment of such a project: but fate ordered otherwise.

On the 17th, the army marched in the direction of Mount St. Jean.

On the 18th, the battle began at one o'clock, and though the bulletin, which details it, makes no mention of me, it is not necessary for me to mention that I was engaged in it. Lieutenant General Count Drouet has already spoken of that battle, in the House of Peers. His narration is accurate, with the exception of some important facts which he has passed over in silence, or of which he was ignorant, and which it is now my duty to declare. About seven o'clock in the evening, after the most frightful carnage which I have ever witnessed, General Labedoyere came to me with a message from the Emperor, that Marshal Grouchy had arrived on our right, and attacked the left of the English and Prussians united. This General Officer, in riding along the lines, spread this intelligence among the soldiers, whose courage and devotion remained unshaken, and who gave new proofs of them at that moment, in spite of the fatigue which they experienced. Immediately after, what was my astonishment, I should rather say indignation, when I learned, that so far from Marshal Grouchy having arrived to support us, as the whole army had been assured, between forty and fifty thousand Prussians attacked our extreme right, and forced it to retire!

Whether the Emperor was deceived with regard to the time when the Marshal could support him, or whether the march of the Marshal was retarded by the efforts of the enemy, longer than was calculated upon, the fact is, that at the moment when his arrival was announced to us, he was only at Wavre upon the Dyle, which to us was the same as if he had been a hundred leagues from the field of battle.

A short time afterwards, I saw four regiments of the middle guard, conducted by the Emperor, arriving. With these troops, he wished to renew the attack, and to penetrate the centre of the enemy. He ordered me to lead them on; generals, officers, and soldiers all displayed the greatest intrepidity; but this body of troops was too weak to resist, for a long time, the forces opposed to it by the enemy, and it was soon necessary to renounce the hope which this attack had, for a few moments, inspired. General Friant had been struck with a ball by my side, and I myself had my horse killed, and fell under it. The brave men who will return from this terrible battle will, I hope, do me the justice to say, that they saw me on foot with sword in hand during the whole of the evening, and that I only quitted the scene of carnage among the last, and at the moment when retreat could no longer be prevented. At the same time, the Prussians continued their offensive movements, and our right sensibly retired; the English advanced in their turn. There remained to us still four squares of the Old Guard to protect the retreat. These brave grenadiers, the choice of the army, forced successively to retire, yielded ground foot by foot, till overwhelmed by numbers, they were almost entirely annihilated. From that moment, a retrograde movement was declared, and the army formed nothing but a confused mass. There was not however, a total rout, nor the cry of *sauve qui peut*, as has been calumniously stated in the bulletin. As for myself, constantly in the rear-guard, which I followed on foot, having all my horses killed, worn out with fatigue, covered with contusions, and having no longer strength to march, I owe my life to a corporal who supported me on the road, and did not abandon me during the retreat. At eleven at night I found Lieutenant General Lefebvre Desnouettes; and one of his officers, Major Schmidt, had the generosity to give me the only horse that remained to him. In this manner I arrived at Marchienne-au-pont at four o'clock in the morning, alone, without any officers of my staff, ignorant of what had become of the Emperor, who, before the end of the battle, had entirely disappeared, and who, I was allowed to believe, might be either killed or taken prisoner. General Pamphele Lacroix, chief of the staff of the second corps, whom I found in this city, having told me that the Emperor was at Charleroi, I was led to suppose that his Majesty was going to put himself at the head of Marshal Grouchy's corps, to cover the Sambre, and to facilitate to the troops the means of rallying towards Avesnes, and, with this persuasion, I went to Beaumont; but parties of cavalry following on too near, and having already intercepted the roads of Maubeuge and Philippeville, I became sensible of the total impossibility of arresting a single soldier on that point to oppose the progress of the victorious enemy. I continued my march upon Avesnes, where I could obtain no intelligence of what had become of the Emperor.

In this state of matters, having no knowledge of his Majesty nor of the Major-General, confusion increasing every moment, and, with the exception of some fragments of regiments of the guard and of the line, every one following his own inclination, I determined immediately to go to Paris by St. Quentin, to disclose, as quickly as possible, the true state of affairs to the Minister of War, that he might send to the army some fresh troops, and take the measures which circumstances rendered necessary. At my arrival at Bourget, three leagues from Paris, I learned that the emperor had passed there at nine o'clock in the morning.

Such, M. le Duc, is a history of the calamitous campaign.

Now I ask those who have survived this fine and numerous army, how I can be accused of the disasters of which it has been the victim, and of which your military annals furnish no example. I have, it is said, betrayed my country—I who, to serve it, have shown a zeal which I perhaps have carried to an extravagant height: but this calumny is supported by no fact, by no circumstance. But how can these odious reports, which spread with frightful rapidity, be arrested? If, in the researches which I could make on this subject, I did not fear almost as much to discover as to be ignorant of the truth, I would say, that all was a tendency to convince that I have been unworthily deceived, and that it is attempted to cover, with the pretence of treason, the faults and extravagancies of this campaign; faults which have not been avowed in the bulletins that have appeared, and against which I in vain raised that voice of truth which I will yet cause to resound in the House of Peers. I expect, from the candour of your Excellency, and from your indulgence to me, that you will cause this letter to be inserted in the Journal, and give it the greatest possible publicity.

MARSHAL PRINCE OF MOSKWA.

Paris, June 26, 1815.

FINIS.

James Clarke,
Printer, Edinburgh.

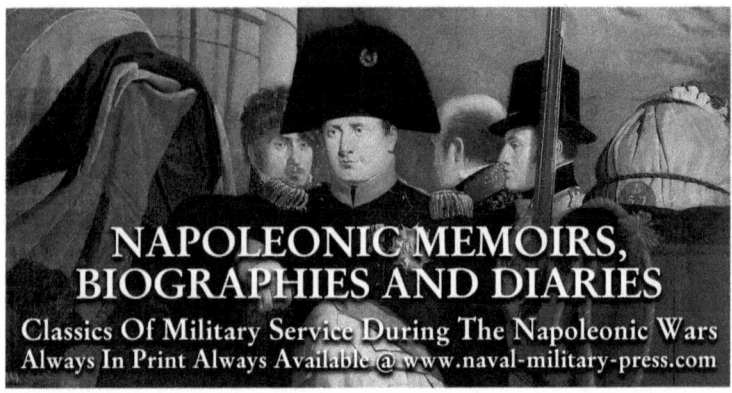

NAPOLEONIC MEMOIRS, BIOGRAPHIES AND DIARIES
Classics Of Military Service During The Napoleonic Wars
Always In Print Always Available @ www.naval-military-press.com

A MEMOIR OF THE SERVICES OF LIEUTENANT - GENERAL SIR SAMUEL FORD WHITTINGHAM K.C.B., K.C.H., G.C.F.

Colonel of the 71st Highland light infantry.
Derived chiefly from his own letters and from those of distinguished contemporaries

Important and voluminous memoirs, with records of service including the disastrous attack on Buenos Aires, much on the Peninsular War and concluding with campaigns in India. Whittingham was a fine and brave officer, severely wounded at Talavera. The modern reader will find much of value in this reprint of the second and best revised edition of this core reference book.

9781474540773

ROUGH SKETCHES OF THE LIFE OF AN OLD SOLDIER

during a service in the West Indies; at the siege of Copenhagen in 1807; in the Peninsula and the south of France in the campaigns from 1808 to 1814, with the Light division; in the Netherlands in 1815; including the battles of Quatre Bras and Waterloo: with a slight sketch of the three years passed by the army of occupation in France, etc."

Lieutenant-Colonel Jonathan Leach with this memoir offers a first-hand account of the newly formed light infantry division, at an interesting and turbulent time for the division. Leach offers here an unbroken narrative; almost every scene recounted in this work was one to which he was an eyewitness and recorded in his journal. For other scenes, the author utilised the logbooks of his brother officers.

9781474540919

THE AUTOBIOGRAPHY OF SERGEANT WILLIAM LAWRENCE. A HERO OF THE PENINSULAR AND WATERLOO CAMPAIGNS.

Sergeant Lawrence's memoir is one of the most important sources of information on life in the ranks during the Napoleonic Wars. Lawrence enlisted in the 40th Regt., served in the River Plate expedition, Peninsular 1809-14 (inc. Talavera, Busaco, Badajoz, Vitoria &c.) & Waterloo campaigns.

9781474540155

John Spencer Cooper's ROUGH NOTES OF SEVEN CAMPAIGNS IN PORTUGAL, SPAIN, FRANCE AND AMERICA DURING THE YEARS 1809-15

An exceptional first-hand account written by a Sergeant of the 7th Royal Fusiliers who served and fought in most of the famous battles and sieges of the Peninsular Campaign during the Napoleonic Wars, including such battles as Talavera, Busaco, Albuera, Ciudad Rodrigo, Badajoz, Vittoria and the battles for the Pyrenees.

9781474539173

RECOLLECTIONS OF MY MILITARY LIFE 1806-1808
Military Engineering During The Peninsular War

A two Volume military autobiography penned by a rather colourful officer of the Royal Engineers who was part of the Gibraltar garrison, and saw active service during the Peninsular War. Serving as a Captain George Landmann was present at the battle of Roleia, reconnoitred the field of Vimeiro, and commanded his corps at the battle. He completed many military engineering constructions, including a flying bridge at Villa Velha, he also reported on fortifications, that led to vigourous efforts being made to defend them.

9781783317950

MEMOIRS OF SIR LOWRY COLE

The author of these memoirs was commissioned a cornet in 1787 and served in the East Indies, Ireland and Egypt before taking part in almost all the battles of the Peninsular War as commander of the 4th division. He retired as a full General in 1830.

9781845749873

THE LIFE AND CAMPAIGNS OF FIELD-MARSHAL PRINCE BLÜCHER,

of Wahlstatt, from the Period of his Birth and First Appointment in the Prussian Service, down to his Second Entry into Paris, in 1815. This new edition of 'The Life and Campaigns of Field-Marshal Prince Blücher' contains every word of the original book – more than 400 pages – complete with the original pagination, small battle plans with coloured troop positions, a map of Germany with coloured outlines, a good index completes this excellent reprint.
"Forwards!" he was quoted as saying when arriving on the field of Waterloo in the late afternoon. "I hear you say it's impossible, but it has to be done! I have given my promise to Wellington, and you surely don't want me to break it? Push yourselves, my children, and we'll have victory!"
9781783317943

PASSAGE DE LA BERESINA
26-27-28- et 29th Novembre 1812

Dramatic and historic eyewitness account in French of the crossing of the Beresina - the culminating action of Napoleon's retreat from Moscow. This facsimile document comes with an English translation of the text.
9781845748807

RECOLLECTIONS OF THE EVENTFUL LIFE OF A SOLDIER

This memoir of civilian life in Glasgow and of the Peninsula War tells the early story of a private who served with Picton's Division, left the army in 1814, and ended his military career as a recruiting officer for the East India Company.
9781845747596

JOURNAL OF A SOLDIER OF THE 71ST, OR GLASGOW REGIMENT, FROM 1806 TO 1815

This is the remarkable military memoir of an anonymous soldier of the Glasgow Regiment who took part in several of the disasters - as well as many of the triumphs - of the Napoleonic wars.
9781845747510

www.ingramcontent.com/pod-product-compliance
Lightning Source LLC
Chambersburg PA
CBHW060520100426
42743CB00009B/1394